Making sense of emotional intelligence

Second Edition

Prof M Higgs
Prof V Dulewicz

eiQ
DULEWICZ & HIGGS

DREVISOR®

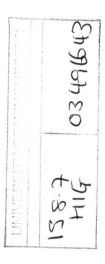

Published by PreVisor, Arlington Square, Downshire Way, Bracknell, Berkshire, RG12 1WA.

Copyright © 2002 PreVisor Inc., Prof M Higgs & Prof V Dulewicz

Printed in Great Britain

Code: 0090008636 / EAN: 978-07087-03670   5(3.11)

Contents

List of Tables

List of Figures

Foreword to the Second Edition

Since we produced the first edition of *Making Sense of Emotional Intelligence* there has been a huge amount of publicity, academic debate and disagreement over the validity, robustness and applicability of the concept. Indeed, on many occasions we have been involved in this debate. However, while the debate among academics has raged, the concept has moved from being one of national media attention to an emerging framework and tool used by HR practitioners. In both academic and practitioner journals the debate centres around two core themes:

- Is the concept anything new?
- Is there any valid evidence for the claims?

We believe that, to an extent, this debate continues to rage around some fundamental misunderstandings about the nature of the concept. In terms of solid evidence for the associated claims we believe that many of the empirical studies carried out in the UK have not been taken into consideration by the international community of occupational psychologists and (to a lesser extent) HR practitioners. We have continued to work with the concept on a research basis and have tried to keep our research in line with both the continuing academic debate and burgeoning academic claims.

We believe that for many practitioners there is still a large degree of confusion around this topic and a need to 'make sense' of the debate. This second edition provides further empirical input to the debate and also explores some of the more recent claims for its importance (e.g. the relationship between EI and leadership) from both a theoretical and research basis.

Overall, we continue to maintain that the concept has much practical value, which is grounded in research and can be a valuable tool in the armoury of those involved with understanding and managing the behaviour of people within today's organisations.

Malcolm Higgs and Victor Dulewicz
Henley, July 2002

Preface and Acknowledgements

Since first encountering the term emotional intelligence we have been intrigued by the following questions:

- Is the concept anything new?
- Is there strong evidence to demonstrate its value in a work context?
- Can emotional intelligence be measured?
- Can emotional intelligence be developed?

When we started investigating the concept and exploring the existing literature we found that not only was it difficult to answer these questions, but the way in which people interpreted the concept seemed to be widely different. Our conclusions from the literature were reinforced in discussions with colleagues. Furthermore, the way in which the media had latched onto the concept has further highlighted apparently differing views on what the term means.

The lack of clarity over the answer to the questions we raised, and the evident confusion over the nature of emotional intelligence, led us into a research journey aimed at resolving the contradictions and ambiguities we had encountered. The first edition of this book was intended to describe our journey, set out *our* answers to the questions we raise and, hopefully, provide clarity in relation to the nature of the concept of emotional intelligence. This second edition updates some of our original work based on extensive research findings. In addition, it presents some refinements to our original models and ideas. As we have progressed on the journey we have found that discussing our findings has continued to be helpful to those who are interested in the concept. Furthermore, we have found that in discussing research results with colleagues and practitioners in organisations, the meaning of emotional intelligence has become clearer and its implications widely understood.

As with any venture into relatively new areas, the attempt to answer some questions has raised others. In this book we hope that we have provided answers to our initial questions. However, we also hope that in doing this we have raised further questions which will help focus further research, with a view to contributing to a more far reaching understanding of the nature of emotional intelligence and its significance to both organisations and individuals.

Having now completed the second edition of the book we have had the chance to reflect on those who have helped us on our way. First we should thank both of our wives (Jacki and Jackie) for their contributions, not only in the 'traditional' way of providing support, encouragement and forbearance, but also for a more active involvement in providing feedback on earlier drafts, in drawing our attention to recent writing on the topic and suggesting its relevance to our teaching and consulting work. Their interest was sustained beyond initiating our work in this area, into acting as challengers and indeed reviewers of our progress.

Having encouraged us to start out on the journey, we need to thank our colleagues at Henley Management College for their support, interest and encouragement. This took the form of not only verbal support but, for many, taking the time and effort to persuade their students to participate in our early research. A number of these colleagues provided further support in reviewing and commenting, most helpfully, on early drafts of the manuscript. It is always difficult to decide on who should receive specific acknowledgement at this stage. However, among our colleagues we feel two should be mentioned specifically. Firstly, Dr Patricia Bossons who went through an early draft and provided very welcome encouragement and helpful suggestions. Secondly, Professor Gareth Jones, who freely gave his agreement to use the organisational culture model developed by himself and Professor Rob Goffee (see **chapter 10**). Gareth also provided invaluable insights into the way in which we could express our views on the cultural links with emotional intelligence in an effective and robust way. Finally, in terms of colleagues, we want to thank our secretary, Carol Collis, for her help in preparing the manuscripts.

Much of the work described in this book results from studies we have conducted in a wide range of organisations. We would like to thank all those who worked with us on these projects.

The foregoing acknowledgements relate to the conceptual content of the book. We have to say that our original publisher Dr Sue Reed provided much of the motivation for us to capture our research and turn it into both the psychometric assessment published by PreVisor and the book itself. PreVisor has continued this work and encouraged us to revise and update the book.

Malcolm Higgs and Victor Dulewicz
July 2002

Why is Emotional Intelligence So Important?

Introduction

During the last few years we have seen an enormous amount of interest in the idea of emotional intelligence. The view that, other things being equal, emotional intelligence accounts for the difference between personal success and failure is one that has captured the interest of the media. There have been numerous articles in leading newspapers which attempt to explain the performance, perceptions and, indeed, peccadilloes of leading politicians in terms of their possession or lack of this 'most desirable' characteristic. The problems of the former US President, Bill Clinton, have been examined in terms of his lack of emotional intelligence while the success of the current British Prime Minister, Tony Blair, has been attributed to his high level of emotional intelligence. Newspaper articles have attempted to show that the 'new millennium' requires a different type of business leader; one who possesses the new quality of emotional intelligence.

While it is possible to attribute this phenomenon to the journalistic powers of the 'father of emotional intelligence', Daniel Goleman, this explanation is far too simplistic. In his seminal book, *Emotional Intelligence – Why it Matters More Than IQ*, Goleman has presented us with an established stream of research and literature which relates to the topic. However well-constructed, the presentation of a concept needs more to achieve the current level of interest than 'spin'. The concept, its presentation and the need for both, have to coincide in order to generate such a high level of professional, academic, business and public interest. Thus, the question arises as to the circumstances which are 'conspiring' to generate the situation in which an idea is seen so widely as offering explanations for our everyday experiences.

It is the resonance between the concept of emotional intelligence with our daily experience which accounts for the level of interest in its nature and measurement. Whether we are a practising manager, academic or member of the public, we can all point to clear (and often impressive) examples of situations in which one individual has all of the rationally determined characteristics which *should* predict success, but fails to realise his potential due to his lack of an 'indefinable' personal quality. In many cases we explain this in the phrase 'they may be very bright, but they don't have much common sense'. This factor appears to be supported, if not explained, through research by such eminent academics as Bahn and Belbin who have demonstrated that the cumulative addition of intelligence (as measured by various IQ tests) fails to explain differences in individual and team performance once a threshold level has been achieved. In a broader context, Goleman has summarised research from educationalists which demonstrates that school and early academic attainments (in a broad context) are dependent on more than 'traditional' measures of intelligence.

The core proposition of the emotional intelligence 'school' is that **life success** requires a combination of an average level of 'traditional' intelligence with above average levels of 'emotional intelligence'. This proposition certainly provides a potential explanation for the findings of Bahn who demonstrated that, beyond a certain level, 'traditional' intelligence (as measured by IQ tests) tended to be counter-productive in terms of broad measures of performance. The research into intelligence as a predictor of performance has generally shown that IQ measures do not account for a large proportion of variance. There is general agreement (from the research) that only around 20 to 25 per cent of the variance in individual attainment and performance in a work context can be explained by differences in IQ. Having said this, the explanation of such a level of variance is considerable. However, as with any indicator of success, the focus tends to switch to what predicts the unexplained, and larger, proportion of variance. There is nothing new about the limitations of IQ in predicting an adequate amount of variation in the 'performance' of individuals when assessed in a broader 'real-world' context. The antecedents of exploring a broader view of individual characteristics which account for differences in individual success go back to the 1920s. Thorndike addressed this issue and proposed a concept of 'social intelligence' which in combination with intellectual intelligence would account for differentiation in individual success. The elements which Thorndike included in his 'social intelligence' bear an uncanny resemblance to current thinking on emotional intelligence. However, Thorndike's thinking was not developed due to the challenges surrounding the emotive nature/nurture arguments and the growth and dominance of behaviouralists in the field of psychology at the time. In an educational context, the concepts of Thorndike were revisited and explored in Gardner's work and further reinforced in Goleman's drawing together of such psychologically-based research and physiological developments in our understanding of the functioning of the human brain.

The reader may be forgiven for saying 'This is all very interesting, but how can it help me in my role of working within an organisational context?' Indeed, Goleman's original work, and the stream of literature which it has prompted, attempts to address this question. However, in attempting to explore the relationship between the concept of emotional intelligence and organisations the focus has been primarily on the individual's progress in the organisational context. In this arena research presents us with a significant volume of anecdotal and case study data which appears to demonstrate the organisational significance of emotional intelligence. In addition, in an environment in which individuals are told (as a part of the new psychological contract) to take accountability for, and ownership of, their own career management, any information which will assist with this is bound to be widely welcomed. Emotional intelligence provides one further, and potentially powerful, addition to the data available to individuals in such a context.

The needs of the individual within a significantly changed organisational context, may explain a degree of interest in the concept of emotional intelligence, given its apparent predictive validity in terms of personal 'success'. In this context, the definition of 'success' is fairly broad and focuses on individual, rather than organisational needs. In the early 21st century, this focus alone would not account for the predominance that the concept has apparently achieved. While, from an organisational perspective, emotional intelligence, with its focus on the individual's role in *managing* his own career, may align with the new version of the psychological contract and may be appealing, it is not sufficiently compelling to account for the level of corporate, as well as individual, interest in the concept. In order to understand the level of corporate interest it is necessary to reflect on the broader changes in organisational theory, new strategic paradigms and perceptions of the drivers of sustainable competitive advantage in what is widely agreed to be a more volatile, unpredictable and fiercely competitive world.

In the search for strategies which will deliver sustainable competitive advantage many organisations have become interested in research which focuses on 'emotional' rather than 'rational' factors. This shift is epitomised by the success of the concepts proposed by Collins and Porras in their book *Built to Last* which emphasises the enduring dominance of emotional rather than rational components of organisational 'strategy'. The concept has been accepted by many, but is seen to be challenging in moving from conceptual acceptance to practical implementation. **Figure 1.1** illustrates the need to integrate the rational and emotional aspects of strategy and its implementation in order to achieve sustained competitive advantage.

Figure 1.1: The Rational and Emotional Aspects of Corporate Strategy

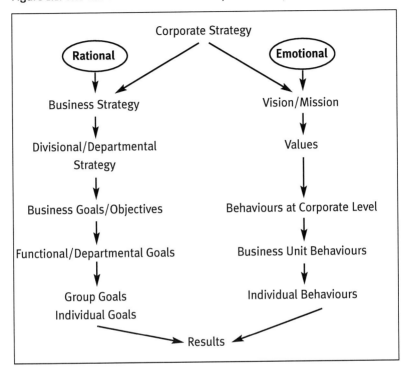

In looking at this model it is evident that much of the historic approach to developing competitive advantage, and helping managers to deliver this, has focused on the 'rational' route. The dominance of the rational focus in organisations can be traced back to the 19th century sociologist Weber, who proposed rational bureaucracy as a means of ensuring that organisational decisions and actions were objective and free from emotional sway. From a managerial perspective this viewpoint became institutionalised following the work and writings of Frederick Taylor in the 1920s. He initiated the concept of 'scientific management'. These two influences have, despite many subsequent developments in management thinking and practice, ensured that rationality is deeply embedded in the organisational psyche. The 'emotional' route has traditionally been perceived as dysfunctional to organisational performance. Attempts to explore and redress the imbalance through focus on vision and values have been popular, but perceived as too 'soft' to deliver real and sustainable competitive advantage expressed through sustainable bottom-line results. Examples provided by Collis and Porras (e.g. Hewlett Packard) demonstrate the link between the rational and emotional elements of business and the value of this in delivering competitive advantage.

At an individual level, Goleman proposed that an average level of IQ and high level of emotional intelligence is a formula for success. The work of Collins and Porras suggests an organisational parallel to this individual success equation (i.e. a balance between rational and emotional elements of business strategies leads to success).

Organisations are now seeking new paradigms to help them succeed and prosper. The rhetoric of 'people provide our competitive success' has to be translated into realistic policies, practices and processes. Not only are organisations operating in increasingly volatile, competitive and global environments, they recognise that these environments are more complex. Winners in this context appear to operate in different ways. Within the UK, the success of entrepreneurial organisations such as Virgin, led by Richard Branson, have focused interest on leaders and leadership and their impact on organisational performance. The inability of research to offer consistent, valid and reliable guidance on leadership qualities and behaviour has created a vacuum in knowledge and models which can explain and provide a basis for replicating the success of organisations such as Virgin. The concept of emotional intelligence deals with perceptions of the characteristics of successful leaders such as Branson and excites interest in increasing the understanding of its reliability, nature and applicability as an organisational development tool capable of adding real value.

Most of the literature on emotional intelligence was initially focused on individual and 'life success'. There were a number of small studies and case descriptions which gave a tantalising view of the potential value the concept had for organisations. Over the last few years, prompted by the widespread interest and initial positive findings, there has been a significant growth in studies designed to examine emotional intelligence in an organisational context. These studies have confirmed the relationship between emotional intelligence and individual success. However, they have also shown strong relationships with individual performance, stress tolerance, morale and job satisfaction. The studies have been remarkably consistent across a wide range of roles and organisational settings. Similar pictures emerge from mixed samples of managers, purchasing managers, sales staff, team leaders, air traffic controllers and even call centre employees. Given this evidence it is clear that organisations have the potential to enhance performance either by using emotional intelligence as a selection criterion or working to develop the existing employees (or, indeed, a combination of the two). The range of benefits claimed (based largely on anecdotes and small scale case histories) for focusing on emotional intelligence include:

- Improved leadership
- More effective handling and resolution of disputes
- More effective development of teamworking
- Improved negotiations
- More cost-effective decision-making
- Better quality problem-solving and decision-making.

This is a powerful list of potential benefits which, for many organisations, goes to the heart of their ability to achieve a sustainable competitive advantage. While we believe that the evidence for performance-related benefits is relatively strong, the evidence for other benefits on this list is still emerging. In particular, the claim for the links between emotional intelligence and leadership has grown, both in volume and intensity. This important area is explored in some detail in **chapter 8**. A key issue in the debate around emotional intelligence is the extent to which it is feasible to develop an individual's emotional intelligence. This issue is core to our thinking about applications of the concept and is one that we explore in detail in **chapter 7**.

While the case for emotional intelligence, to a large extent, was based on theoretical arguments, anecdotal and derivative evidence, the authors have conducted systematic research in a business context which supports other evidence and arguments. This has shown the validity of the concept when predicting individual success, the potential to measure the 'trait' and the possibility of developing this important set of skills and behaviours.

In subsequent chapters we will explore and discuss the nature of emotional intelligence, how it can be developed and the organisational implications in terms of nurturing, promoting and exploiting this personal attribute to achieve enduring competitive advantage. We will also support the claims for the benefits of focusing on emotional intelligence. Throughout, we will try to balance the potential of the concept with the evidence available. We believe that it is vital to ensure that there is real evidence to support claims rather than persuasive arguments and rhetoric alone.

What is Emotional Intelligence?

Chapter 1 highlighted the growing interest in the concept of emotional intelligence and its potential value to both individuals and organisations. In this chapter we will explore what the concept really means. It is important to understand that the concept is not simply about being a nice, warm, 'cuddly' person – a common concept featured in the growing media coverage. We hope to show that, while interpersonal sensitivity is an important component of emotional intelligence, there is also a 'harder', outcome-focused, component to the overall concept.

General Definitions and Terminology

The literature relating to emotional intelligence contains a range of terminology which can be confusing. This includes:

- Emotional Intelligence

- Emotional Literacy

- Emotional Quotient

- Personal Intelligence

- Social Intelligence

- Interpersonal Intelligence.

In essence, a common explanation is that the authors are attempting to develop and label a concept which captures the elements of an individual's personality and behaviours which are **not** concerned with the rational, analytical or intellectual domains. One author (Martinez) reflects this view in a definition of emotional intelligence as:

'*... an array of non-cognitive skills, capabilities and competencies that influence a person's ability to cope with environmental demands and pressures.*' Martinez (1977), p.72.

This definition may appeal to psychologists and other academics but it needs to be 'unpacked' to ascertain its practical meaning. Daniel Goleman, who has done so much to bring the concept to the attention of a wider public, has provided a very useful initial framework for understanding what is meant by emotional intelligence. In a conference presentation in 1997 he commented that emotional intelligence is about:

- Knowing what you are feeling and being able to handle those feelings without having them swamp you;

- Being able to motivate yourself to get jobs done, be creative and perform at your peak; and

- Sensing what others are feeling, and handling relationships effectively.

This summary is the starting point in our explanation of the concept. We will explore this, and other views before presenting our own definition in this chapter.

In attempting to understand emotional intelligence as a concept and consider how it might be of value in a business environment three important questions need to be answered. These are:

- What is emotional intelligence?
- Can it be measured?
- Can it be developed?

To a large extent these three questions have been highlighted in existing literature. However, they have not, as yet, been brought together in a way which helps the practitioner evaluate the value of the concept in a work context. The three questions can be seen as being closely interwoven with the measurement and development flowing from the definition and being interactive. This relationship is summarised in **Figure 2.1** with the key terminology being:

Emotional Intelligence. This term refers to the overall concept as defined by Martinez and encompasses the concepts of Social Intelligence, Interpersonal Intelligence and Personal Intelligence.

Emotional Literacy. This is used either as a synonym for Emotional Intelligence or as a process involved in developing it. However, it makes more sense as a term to describe the development of emotional intelligence.

Emotional Quotient (EQ). This is an alternative to emotional intelligence. It is more commonly used to describe an individual's emotional intelligence. In much of the literature EQ is positioned as being analogous to the common measure of 'rational intelligence', IQ.

Figure 2.1: Dynamics of Emotional Intelligence

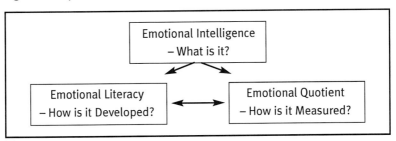

Building an Understanding

Attempts to describe and understand any aspect of personality or behaviour are bedevilled with broad definitions which are capable of very different interpretations. To be useful within an organisational context, the concept has to be taken to a level of detail which will assist in consistent interpretation, and assist in formulating ways of measuring and developing it.

Building an understanding of the full nature of emotional intelligence requires spending a little time reflecting on the background to the concept. This was mentioned briefly in **chapter 1**, but it is worth exploring it in a little more depth in order to build a clear picture of what emotional intelligence really means.

The roots of the development of the concept of emotional intelligence appear to lie in the apparent inability of measures of 'rational thinking', e.g. IQ, Standard Attainment Test (SAT) scores, grades, etc. to predict individual success in life. Goleman maintains that, in general terms, research indicates that IQ at best contributes about 20 per cent of the factors. This is certainly in line with conclusions drawn by researchers who have a *prima facie* commitment to the primacy of IQ. For example, Hernstein and Murray in a study of the relationship between IQ and 'broad' measures of life success concluded:

> *'... The link between test scores and those (broad) achievements is dwarfed by the totality of other characteristics which are brought to life.'*

In an organisational, rather than educational, setting, Bahn reported a study which was designed to assess the validity of IQ tests in predicting executive or management competency. He concluded that leaders tended to be more intelligent than the average group member, but were not the most intelligent. His review of the studies in this field indicated a certain minimum base line IQ as being necessary for effective performance. However, he comments that:

' If we use intelligence test scores as simply one of several indicators of competency, they can make a valuable contribution to the critically important assessments involved in executive selection and promotion. Test scores do not constitute comprehensive or final judgements about a person's capacity ... An outstanding executive is much more than a highly intelligent individual.'

The search for characteristics, other than IQ, which adequately explain variations in success is by no means new. In the 1920s, Thorndike developed the concept of social intelligence as a means of explaining variations in outcome measures not accounted for by IQ. This early venture into the field of emotional intelligence was somewhat stifled by the predominance of the behaviourists in the 1920s and 1930s and the subsequent focus on cognitive psychology. The interest in a broader view of the totality of intelligence was resurrected by researchers such as Gardner and Hatch in the late 1980s. They developed and explored the concept of multiple intelligences. The spectrum of intelligences proposed by Gardner was examined in conjunction with a measure of IQ and no significant relationships were found. This led to a conclusion that the 'other' intelligences proposed by Gardner were a distinctly different construct from IQ.

In one study, people were asked to describe an 'intelligent person'. Among the main attributes was 'practical people skills'. One of the conclusions from this study was that practical people skills which are valued in the workplace include the type of sensitivity which enables managers to pick up tacit messages. Studies such as these re-awoke interest in Thorndike's social intelligence idea. Two recent researchers, Mayer and Stevens, identified that people may be grouped into three distinctive categories based on their styles and strategies for attending to and dealing with their emotions. These they suggested are:

- **Self-aware:** aware of their moods as they are experiencing them; autonomous and sure of their own boundaries; possessing a positive outlook on life; mindful and capable of managing their emotions.

- **Engulfed:** feeling swamped by their own emotions and helpless in terms of escaping from them; moods and emotions take charge of behaviour; unaware of their feelings with little control over their emotional lives.

- **Accepting:** having clarity about their own feelings; accepting of their moods and unmotivated or unwilling to try to change them.

An example of such additional emotional abilities is that of **empathy**. Evidence supports the view that those people who have well-developed empathy tend to be emotionally better adjusted, more sensitive, more popular and more outgoing.

Given the range of literature which explores emotional intelligence, it is important for both measurement and development purposes, to develop a detailed picture of the concept, built on common elements in the literature research. We have identified that the core, common, components of emotional intelligence are:

- Self-awareness
- Emotional management and resilience
- Self-motivation
- Empathising with others
- Managing relationships with others
- Making decisions in complex interpersonal situations
- Being conscientious and behaving with integrity.

We will begin by examining these elements in more detail before describing the components of our model of emotional intelligence in **chapter 5**.

Self-awareness

Self-awareness relates to an individual's self-knowledge. This encompasses the individual's tendency to know and be in touch with their feelings and to understand their feelings and emotions. Highly self-aware individuals tend to recognise feelings as they happen and relate their personal feelings to the context in which they are working. Self-awareness also allows individuals to make a realistic appraisal of their own strengths and thus they are able to make the most of them. They can use these feelings with confidence in a decision-making context.

Self-awareness in action

You are asked to make a presentation to senior management on a topic related to your area of specialism. You are aware that you must make a good impression as it may impact on your career, but also that you tend to go into a lot of detail to ensure that others gain a clear view of your specialist knowledge. You recognise that you have a fear of appearing inadequately prepared and being labelled as a 'back room expert'. You genuinely believe that you have a good grasp of your topic, but know that you are not a 'charismatic' presenter. You know that you are much better in an open discussion of the topic and its implications and feel more comfortable doing this. In deciding how to approach the presentation you take account of these feelings and decide to use a short initial presentation with the bulk of the time being allocated to discussion or a question and answer session.

Emotional Management and Resilience

This is an awareness of one's own feelings and emotions balanced with an ability to avoid becoming 'swamped' by them. In other words even when aware of personal feelings of cynicism or frustration, in a work context, one can still make effective decisions and fulfil accountabilities. This needs an ability to maintain a focus on results or actions while also being able to express personal feelings effectively. This component of emotional intelligence needs the ability to recognise both the positive and negative impact of one's own feelings and emotions in a work context and to control these in a way which ensures that both organisational and personal goals are satisfied – the ability to perform an emotional balancing act between feelings and results.

Emotional Management and Resilience in action

You are asked to implement a reorganisation of your department which will reduce its apparent importance in the organisation. You are aware that this will be damaging to the careers of a number of very talented specialists in the department. From a personal point of view you are concerned that the move will potentially limit your own future career. At the same time you recognise the logical argument for the reorganisation. You recognise and acknowledge all of these concerns. However, you prepare an effective implementation plan to present to, and discuss with, your boss. Having prepared the plan you reflect on its implications, particularly for you personally, and decide to present your concerns to your boss at the same time. You set out to present the plan and to ensure that you have an opportunity to discuss your feelings and ways in which these may be addressed in the same meeting.

Self-motivation

Within the various descriptions of emotional intelligence a strong common element relating to personal motivation arises. Daniel Goleman illustrates this by applying the concept of 'flow' to major athletes performing at their peak. This draws together ideas about what success will look and feel like together with sustained preparation, both physically and mentally, for achieving this goal. To this 'mind-set' is added a degree of self-confidence and self-belief which is grounded in a realistic appraisal of past performance.

The concept is also associated with the related ideas of drive, energy and the desire to make an impact. This implies a need to balance short-term results with longer-term aspirations and an ability to pursue challenging goals in the face of short-term rejection or challenge.

Self-motivation in action

In pursuing your career you have a clear ambition to become a divisional director within your organisation. You are currently two levels below this. You recognise that to pursue your goal you need to demonstrate that you have an ability to produce creative and innovative solutions to business problems. Recognising this as an important area you have over the last two years undertaken training in creative thinking and consistently applied the learning in a work context. Overall you feel confident that you have really developed the ability to apply creative and innovative approaches to the solution of business problems. Your immediate manager had indeed commented favourably on this in your last appraisal. Two months ago you were asked to lead a new product project team sponsored by a member of the board. You knew that the board member was on the promotions committee and saw this as an opportunity to display a critical competence in support of your aspiration. You applied all of your learning to the project and believed that you had come up with a truly innovative product. When the proposals were presented to the board member they were discussed as being insufficiently innovative to warrant further development. At first you felt bitterly disappointed and questioned your learning and abilities. However, you revisited your goals and decided to re-examine the idea and develop an alternative proposal which you sought and obtained an opportunity to present to the board member. In addition you put yourself forward for involvement in a long-term project team briefed to explore ways of re-inventing the core business of the organisation.

Empathising with Others

This, together with managing relationships with others, would seem to be the 'soft and cuddly' elements of emotional intelligence which are emphasised in media coverage of the concept. However, empathising with others does not mean being indiscriminately nice to others, nor sacrificing one's own needs and interests for those of others. In the context of emotional intelligence this element is more akin to enlightened self-interest than sacrificial altruism. Indeed it combines the ability to sense and understand what others are feeling with the ability to recognise how such feelings may conflict with organisational or situational requirements. Empathising with others encompasses a complex and often contradictory set of behaviours. The ability to recognise and have insight into the needs, motivations and feelings of others, to respond to these and to be able to resolve conflict between individual, group and organisational needs represents a high level of interpersonal skills and behaviours. In essence, this component of emotional intelligence requires skills relating to social analysis, deal-making, conflict management, leadership and negotiation. It also requires the ability to convert conflicting and divergent views into creative energy through identifying and making the most of the strengths of others.

Empathising with others in action

You have to explain the proposed organisational changes to the head of a technical function in your department. You reflected on your knowledge of the individual and her background and recognised that she has specialised in this area since graduating ten years ago and that she had also been working with your organisation for those ten years. In recent performance appraisal discussions she had commented on the fact that her contribution seemed to have been valued by the organisation and she anticipated future rewarding growth opportunities. In planning to discuss the proposed re-organisation of the department you spent time thinking about how this member of the team might both feel about the proposal and react to it. In doing this you thought about her background and aspirations and how you might feel and react in a similar situation. Finally you thought about how you would use this information or insight to examine the proposal so that the change might be implemented effectively.

Managing Relationships with Others

This is a very wide-ranging category which encompasses the ability to build rapport in dealing with others, exhibit co-operative behaviours, promote social harmony and display social competencies. However, the ability to manage interpersonal relationships goes well beyond being co-operative and exhibiting social niceties. It is seen as the ability to manage relationships in order to achieve results, and thus entails the ability to persuade others to work as individuals and in teams to achieve important work-related goals. While this aspect of emotional intelligence needs skills which relate to consensus building, it must balance the requirements of a task or project with the needs of the individuals engaged in the work. To a large extent the effective management of relationships with others requires an ability to initiate relationships as well as responding appropriately and productively in the context of existing relationships. This requires the ability to build and maintain networks to deal with work goals, problems and issues.

Managing relationships with others in action

You have built an effective brand management team for your organisation. The brand that you are managing is about to be dramatically repositioned. This will impact not only on your team but also on a related team which had previously managed a complementing brand. These brands are now planned in a position in which your brand is core to the business and the other is a 'decaying' brand. However, you need to persuade the other brand team to maintain commitment to this brand and the associated plans to reposition the brand which you are managing. You approach this by informally meeting with your counterpart to discuss his reactions and feelings. You seek his thoughts and ideas about the way forward and arrange to have joint discussions with a colleague of yours who works in another organisation and has been through a similar experience. You do all of this before sitting down with your counterpart to explore options and ideas which will achieve the business goals and also address as many of his personal concerns as possible.

Making Decisions in Complex Interpersonal Situations

Within the work environment, effective performance requires decision-making which balances the 'hard' and objective information relating to a decision with the 'soft' information relating to the people involved in, and affected by, the decision. The ability to achieve this balance is an important aspect of emotional intelligence. This requires an ability to cope with stress (particularly that arising from emotional conflict) and to maintain and deliver performance when under pressure. It also implies the need to be able to present one's own viewpoint clearly and to be open, honest and direct in discussing the issues relating to a specific problem or decision.

Making decisions in complex interpersonal situations in action

Your department has been working flat out for the past three months to prepare for the implementation of a major systems change. The team leaders who report to you have stated that their team members are complaining about the pressure and excessive hours which they are working. The team leaders have also commented on a slight, but noticeable rise in short periods of sickness in their teams. In informal discussions with the team leaders, on an individual basis, you have sensed that they are also feeling the pressure which, in some cases, is spilling over into their personal lives. You are able to empathise with their position, as you are aware of your own feelings at the moment. You have just been informed that there is a significant modification to be made to the system which will require a further month's intense work for your department and have been asked if you believe your team can deliver to this tight, but critical deadline. You recognise both the importance of the work to the business and the likely impact on you, your team leaders and their team. You reflect on this and, having got the expected input and reactions from the team leaders, decide that you need to agree to deliver. In doing this you recognise that you will have to commit a high level of your time and energy to supporting the team leaders through this difficult period.

Conscientiousness & Integrity

This appears to encompass an individual's ability to accept personal responsibility and accountability for their actions and decisions as well as being open and transparent in their dealings with others. Integrity, in the context of emotional intelligence also encompasses the ability to display a high level of emotional honesty. These behaviours are seen to be important in building trust in working with others. The trust is maintained by the individual's ability to honour and deliver on the commitments which they make. This may be summarised as an ability to match your actions and words in a consistent and sustained manner and to behave ethically in your business life.

Conscientiousness & integrity in action

In the situation described under making decisions in complex interpersonal situations the team leaders as a group approached you. They stated that they needed to take you up on your offer of support. Specifically they wanted you to 'break the news' to the department. In response you discussed your view that they should take accountability for communicating with their team and that you felt bad about intervening in this way as it could undermine their position. However, you also realised that you had made an open commitment to support the team leaders. Therefore, you decided to agree to their request and to ensure that you publicly accepted accountability for the decision. You also decided that, in the meeting with the staff, you would be completely open about the dilemma you faced and the reasoning behind your decision.

In looking over the nature and definition of emotional intelligence outlined above, it is evident that the concept encompasses a range of individual traits, values and behaviours. This would, to a large extent, align with the concept of a competence as it is often used in practice. Indeed there are clear parallels between the drivers of interest in competencies and emotional intelligence, in that both concepts have been developed as an attempt to explain variations in performance which have been inadequately or incompletely addressed by alternative concepts. The drivers for the focus on competencies are often associated with the debatable limitations on the research evidence for a link between personality and job performance. There is, within the literature on emotional intelligence, frequent reference to the nature of the concept being linked to competencies. The way in which some authors have attempted to encapsulate emotional intelligence as 'street smart' appears remarkably close to specific competency labels such as 'organisational savvy' described in the competency literature. The view that emotional intelligence relates to a set of competencies is reinforced by leading authors in the field (including Daniel Goleman), who directly refer to using an understanding of the concept to assist in the improvement of workplace competency. A number of specific competency frameworks include high performing competencies directly aligned to elements of emotional intelligence. For example, Cockerill in identifying high performing competencies, includes a number which touch on emotions (e.g. creating a positive climate). Dulewicz, in exploring and describing his 'supra-competencies', includes a grouping labelled interpersonal competencies, embracing: managing staff; persuasiveness; assertiveness & decisiveness; sensitivity; and oral communication. Overall, the concept of emotional intelligence falls within the thinking on managerial competencies. However, this relationship has not been explored in detail beyond the work described later in this book and some of the more recent work carried out by Daniel Goleman.

In an attempt to pin down the precise nature of emotional intelligence the authors reviewed the literature on the concept (which is summarised above) and examined the detailed content of a range of competency frameworks. They identified that the elements contained within the overall concept of emotional intelligence could be grouped under the following headings (which are broadly similar to those outlined above):

- Self-awareness
- Emotional resilience
- Motivation

- Interpersonal sensitivity

- Influence

- Intuitiveness

- Conscientiousness

The research which underpins this categorisation, and a more detailed exploration of the elements, are dealt with in **chapter 3**.

Tough Love

Reviewing emotional intelligence on a detailed basis demonstrates very clearly that it is far more than merely becoming a warm and engaging person. The concept embraces a wide range of both 'hard' and 'soft' qualities. An individual with a well developed emotional intelligence has the ability to exercise these qualities in a continuing state of tension and balance and is able to continuously monitor and adjust this **balance** to achieve required levels of performance while still able to cope with the personal stresses and pressures this entails. In looking for a relatively simply phrase to summarise what emotional intelligence is all about, the term 'tough love' seems to capture the essence of the concept. At its core there appears to be an ability to maintain a balance between compassion and caring for others with a need to meet the performance goals of a task, job or project.

Achieving this balance is a challenge. It involves working with three distinct, and potentially contradictory groups of personal attributes and abilities. The elements of emotional intelligence can be seen as falling into three categories. These are:

- Drivers of performance (e.g. Motivation)

- Constrainers of actions (e.g. Integrity)

- Facilitators of performance (e.g. Interpersonal sensitivity, Influence)

The interrelationship between these can be summarised diagrammatically as shown in **Figure 2.2**. This framework for understanding the nature and potential for developing emotional intelligence is explored in more detail in **chapters 5** and **7**. However, it also suggests the need for a new definition. We offer the following:

> *'Achieving one's goals through the ability to manage one's own feelings and emotions, to be sensitive to, and influence other key people, and to balance one's motives and drives with conscientious and ethical behaviour.'*

Figure 2.2: Balance in Emotional Intelligence

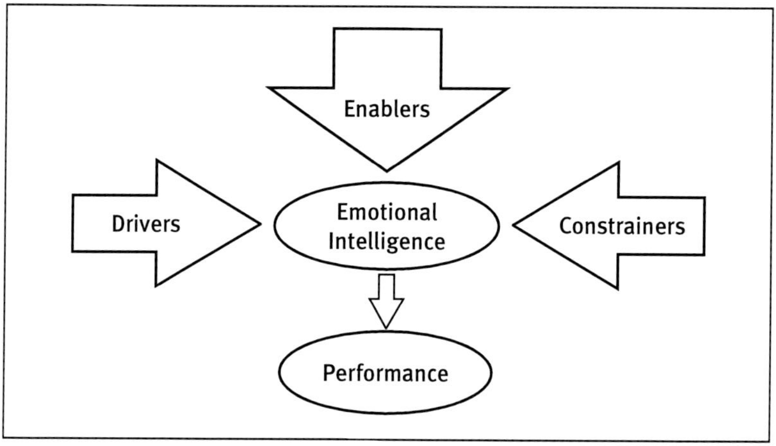

With this level of understanding of the concept of emotional intelligence it is no longer difficult to understand why many individuals with highly developed capabilities in this area are successful, and vice versa. It appears to us that the concept of emotional intelligence has potential significance in examining the success of teams as well as individuals. In addition, the nature of the organisational environment or culture needed to promote and nurture high levels of emotional intelligence is a major area to consider. These topics and their implications are examined in more detail in **chapters 8** and **9**.

Can You Really Measure Emotional Intelligence? Research Studies

Many psychologists say that if you can define a concept, then you can measure it. As we have already said, quoting Goleman's core proposition, it is a combination of intellectual intelligence and emotional intelligence that determines life success. Is it possible to measure emotional intelligence? Experts' views tend to polarise. Many point out that the somewhat more complex and diverse nature of emotional intelligence militates against its effective measurement. In particular, Goleman comments that 'unlike the familiar tests for IQ, there is as yet no single pencil-and-paper test that yields an emotional intelligence score'.

Others tend to endorse this view, suggesting that the term EQ (the measure of emotional intelligence), though snappy, means a lot less than you might think, and is a marketing concept, not a scientific term. An emotional quotient cannot be measured and scored like an intelligence quotient. They believe we can meaningfully speak of EQ as long as we do not claim to be able to measure it precisely.

While the lack of a robust and well-researched method or test for assessing emotional intelligence is widely documented, the search continues for such a measure. Indeed the popular literature and the Internet are full of reports of tests of emotional intelligence, but they lack evidence of rigorous development and examination.

The complex nature of emotional intelligence and its assessment may, indeed, mean that it is difficult to measure by means of a pencil and paper test. However, a starting point for exploring such a test could be via competencies which encompass the more behavioural elements of EI, as well as data from personality questionnaires.

Testing Out Our Ideas – The General Manager Study

We decided to test our definition of emotional intelligence, which derived from our extensive review of the literature from the last 50 years, using competency and personality data from 100 managers. We were interested to see if there was a relationship between a competency-based measure of EI and a measure of success within their organisations over a long period. Similarly, we decided to see if success might also be related to those personality characteristics, measured by two separate questionnaires, we had identified as containing factors which were very similar to EI components.

We were fortunate to have access to a large database containing personality profiles and competency data, derived from self and boss assessments of 100 managers who had attended the Henley Management College's General Management Course in 1988. They had also provided us with information on their responsibilities (their budget, and the number of staff they managed), salary and organisational level (the number of levels below the CEO or MD of their organisation). These managers were contacted seven years later and were asked to provide updated figures. By comparing the two sets of data, we were able to calculate how far the managers had advanced over the intervening period, and then relate this rate of advancement to three measures of EI which were:

(a) Sixteen Personal Competencies relating to factors such as achievement, motivation, sensitivity, resilience, influence, decisiveness, energy and integrity (see **Table 3.1**);

(b) Thirteen factors from the 16PF personality questionnaire which bore some relation to EI constructs; and

(c) Thirteen of the 30 factors from the Occupational Personality Questionnaire which also appeared to be related to EI constructs.

At the outset we were highly sceptical that we would find any relationship between EI and organisational success. This was partly because we were not convinced at the time that EI was relevant for success, but also because we were only using proxy measures of the construct and because long-term studies very rarely show positive results, since so much else occurs in the intervening years to confound any direct relationship. Furthermore, the research reported to date was sparse and far from rigorous. We were therefore extremely surprised to find that there was a clear relationship between the competencies measure of emotional intelligence and our managers' rate of advancement. In contrast, neither of the personality-derived measures showed a direct relationship with success, although the OPQ EI factor score was highly related to the competencies measure of EI factors.

In view of the support we found in the literature for the relevance of intellectual ability ('IQ') to success, we revisited our competency questionnaire to see if any of the items measured intellectual abilities. We discovered that 12 appeared to be measuring a range of primarily intellectual abilities such as analysis, judgment, planning, organising, perspective and creativity. We constructed an 'IQ' score from the performance ratings on these 12 items and found that this was also significantly related to organisational advancement.

We then asked ourselves – what is the nature of the remaining 12 items in the competency questionnaire? They appeared to measure aspects of managerial work, relating to, for example, supervising, delegating, appraising and developing staff; communication (both oral and written); self-management; and business sense. A third aggregate scale was constructed, Managerial Intelligence (MQ), and scores on this scale were also significantly related to the advancement of a sample of managers. A summary of all the EQ, IQ and MQ competencies is presented in **Table 3.1**.

Table 3.1: Personal Competencies Contributing to the EQ, IQ and MQ Scales

I Emotional Intelligence (EQ)	II Intellectual Intelligence (IQ)	III Managerial Intelligence (MQ)
Perceptive Listening Sensitivity Flexibility	Information Collection Problem Analysis Numerical Interpretation Judgment	Delegating Appraising Developing Subordinates
Achievement – Orientation Energy	Detail Consciousness	
Stress Tolerance Resilience	Planning Organising	Oral Expression Oral Presentation Written Presentation
Persuasiveness (& Influence) Negotiating Adaptability	Perspective Organisational Awareness External Awareness	Business Sense Self-Management Reading
Decisiveness Ascendancy Impact Integrity	Creativity Risk-Taking	Initiative Independence Tenacity
Motivating Others Leadership		

Each of our new competency sub-scales appeared to be predicting different aspects of performance relating to advancement. By using other statistical techniques we were able to establish the approximate amount of the total variation of advancement predicted by each. EQ accounted for just over one-third (36%) of the variation, followed by IQ which accounted for another quarter (27%), and finally MQ which explained another 16 per cent of variation on the advancement measure. When all three measures were added up, around three-quarters of the total variation in advancement was explained by (ratings of) performance on the 40 competencies. The remainder is probably down to luck, to being the boss's blue-eyed boy or girl or, more importantly, the culture of the organisation, technical expertise and special knowledge. These results provided support for the widely-held view of experts in this field that intellectual intelligence as well as emotional intelligence is required to be successful in management. We have also shown that, not surprisingly, some specific *managerial competencies* are also needed. The latter would not, of course, be required to be successful in other walks of life.

Designing a tailored EI Questionnaire

While there are numerous IQ tests and managerial competencies questionnaires already available, we felt that there was need for a new tailored questionnaire to measure all aspects of emotional intelligence in detail despite the difficulties outlined above. Our competency-based scale was, after all, only a proxy measure. Therefore, we decided to design a new questionnaire derived from the findings of the extensive work on emotional intelligence over the last 50 years, and then proceeded to test it out on over 200 managers. Extensive analysis of the results demonstrated that EI has seven components or clusters of attributes. The definitions of the elements are as follows:

A Self-awareness

The awareness of one's own feelings and the capability to recognise and manage these feelings in a way which one feels that one can control. This factor includes a degree of self-belief in one's capability to manage one's emotions and to control their impact in a work environment.

B Emotional Resilience

The capability to perform consistently in a range of situations under pressure and to adapt behaviour appropriately. The capability to balance the needs of the situation and task with the needs and concerns of the individuals involved. The capability to retain focus on a course of action or need for results in the face of personal challenge or criticism.

C Motivation

The drive and energy to achieve clear results and make an impact and, also, to balance both short- and long-term goals with a capability to pursue demanding goals in the face of rejection or questioning.

D Interpersonal Sensitivity

The ability to be aware of, and take account of, the needs and perceptions of others when arriving at decisions and proposing solutions to problems and challenges. The capability to build from this awareness and achieve the commitment of others to decisions and action ideas. The willingness to keep open one's thoughts on possible solutions to problems and to actively listen to, and reflect on, the reactions and inputs from others.

E Influence

The capability to persuade others to change a viewpoint based on the understanding of their position and the recognition of the need to listen to this perspective and provide a rationale for change.

F Intuitiveness

The capability to arrive at clear decisions and drive their implementation when presented with incomplete or ambiguous information using both rational and 'emotional' or intuitive perceptions of key issues and implications.

G Conscientiousness

The capability to display clear commitment to a course of action in the face of challenge and to match 'words and deeds' in encouraging others to support the chosen direction. The personal commitment to pursuing an ethical solution to a difficult business issue or problem.

Although these constitute distinct personal characteristics, an individual's score on each element is related to his/her score on the overall EI Measure. These elements are reasonably similar to those identified by Goleman described in **chapter 2**, but they cover the domain in a slightly different way and, most importantly, bring Intuitiveness into the picture. The comparison of the two sets of elements is shown in **Figure 3.1**.

This will be discussed in more detail in the following chapters. At this point, we will describe some interesting findings on links with the other measures, especially, personality characteristics.

Figure 3.1: Comparison of Emotional Intelligence Elements

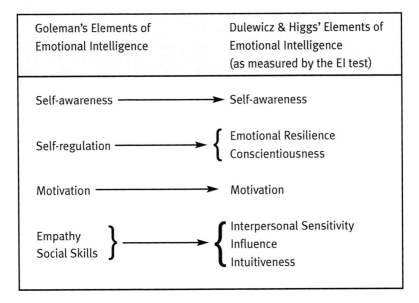

The Big Five (or Six) Dimensions of Personality

An individual's EI is obviously related to his/her personality characteristics. Recent research has identified five or six main dimensions of human personality, four or five of which appear to subsume the seven elements of EI:

1. *Emotional Stability* This covers traits such as being anxious, depressed, angry, emotional, worried and insecure. EI emotional resilience is clearly linked to this broad dimension of personality. Furthermore, EI self-awareness (of one's feelings and capability to manage these) is associated with this dimension, but it is distinctive in that it is concerned with the degree of conscious awareness of, and management of the traits associated with the dimension. EQ makes a unique contribution, because self-awareness is not measured by the most widely used personality questionnaires.

2. *Extraversion-Introversion* Traits such as sociability, gregariousness, assertiveness and talkativeness are embraced by this dimension, none of which appear to be closely linked to EI elements.

3. *Agreeableness* This relates to being courteous, flexible, trusting, good natured, co-operative, forgiving, soft-hearted and tolerant. EI interpersonal sensitivity and influence include elements of both of these two main dimensions of personality. Being primarily outgoing and people-centred, extroverts are more likely to be in a position to show sensitivity and to attempt to influence others. Those who are highly agreeable are more likely to achieve results.

4. *Conscientiousness* The main traits associated with this dimension are dependable, thorough, careful, responsible, organised and planful. However, some psychologists propose an additional subset of motivational traits – hardworking, achievement-oriented and persevering – which taken together

could be viewed as the sixth main dimension of personality. While EI conscientiousness clearly shares many common traits with the main dimension, EI motivation and EI intuitiveness appear to have much more in common with the 'motivational' subset of the main dimension, and would add some support to the argument for making this the sixth major dimension of personality.

5. *Openness to experience* This last dimension is primarily concerned with more cerebral aspects of personality, related to traits such as imaginative, cultured, curious, original, broad-minded, intelligent and artistically sensitive. Since EI is not designed to cover cerebral or intellectual characteristics, this is the second major dimension of personality not covered. It is clearly relevant, however, to the competency-based 'IQ' measure used in our study, which complements 'EQ'.

As we had access to the personality profiles of almost all of our original sample, we were able to explore these hypothesised relationships by relating EI scores to the real personality characteristics. Broadly speaking, we found that 'EI people' (i.e. those with high emotional intelligence) tend to be agreeable. They are socially bold, the sort of person who will talk to complete strangers on a bus or train, and are happy-go-lucky and enthusiastic individuals, the life and soul of any party or social gathering. Those with a high emotional intelligence also tend to be well-adjusted, they are likely to be mature and stable, placid and self-confident, relaxed within themselves and highly controlled.

Those who have high scores on the self-awareness and resilience scales are likely to come out as being well adjusted on all of the emotional stability factors. Those who are high on motivation are likely to be assertive, relaxed and conscientious. In contrast, people with high scores on the sensitivity sub-scale are likely to be mild, accommodating and relaxed, and to exercise high control over their behaviour and emotions. Effective influencers are also likely to be relaxed and self-confident, assertive, enthusiastic and socially bold, as are highly intuitive people. They are likely to be forthright and direct.

Finally, those with high conscientiousness are likely to be relaxed and controlled with high moral standards and principles. They can also at times be rather rule-bound. These results provide support for the links we proposed between the elements of EI and the Big 5 or 6 major dimensions of personality. So our EI elements appear to be well-grounded in the main factors of adult personality, according to current personality theory.

We look next at the biographical characteristics of our original sample of respondents on which, perhaps surprisingly, there were few differences. There were no differences on any of the scales between men and women. This broadly confirms Daniel Goleman's more recent writing on the subject, but remember that all our respondents were managers. We look forward to testing more general groups, to see if our results stand up. The nationality of respondents also showed few differences, apart from the fact respondents from the UK were more intuitive than those from overseas. In addition, managers from the public sector scored higher on conscientiousness than those from the private sector, which was perhaps to be expected.

There was no relationship at all with level in the organisation or responsibilities on any of the elements. However, older managers tended to be more sensitive than younger managers, while those on higher salaries tended to be more intuitive. But overall EI did not appear to be related to, or influenced by, any of these background characteristics.

Probably the most important finding, however, was the fact that there was a very clear relationship between the managers' overall scores on the EI questionnaire and their scores on the competency scale designed to measure EI in our first study. Since the latter had been found to predict managerial advancement over seven years, we were now able to establish a link between 'success' and performance on the EIQ.

The personality profiles are also very valuable for identifying the type of roles which people play when working in groups. Since the team-building implications for applying EI are, in our view, so important, we will cover this subject in **chapter 9**.

The Four Versions of the Emotional Intelligence Questionnaire (EIQ)

The questionnaire described so far was developed to measure EI in managerial roles and has now become known as the Emotional Intelligence Questionnaire: Managerial (EIQ: M). However, in order to examine EI more broadly in the workplace, we went on to develop a questionnaire for use with non-managerial staff, the Emotional Intelligence Questionnaire: General (EIQ: G). This version measures the same elements of emotional intelligence as the managerial version of the questionnaire. It is a parallel version of the instrument in which the wording of items was amended to make some questions easier to understand and to remove any managerial contextualisation from others. However, much of the technical support for the EIQ: G is derived from the extensive research on the managerial version, which will be described later in this chapter.

In view of the nature of the EI construct and, in particular, the importance of Self-awareness, we also saw the need for a version of the EIQ which could be completed by colleagues. Therefore, we modified the items in the original versions of the two self-assessment questionnaires so that they could be rated by a third party. Thus, to date, there are four different versions of EIQ, for managers and other staff, in self and 360° versions.

Studies Showing Support for the Value of EIQ at Work and 'Play'

One important indicator of the soundness of any questionnaire is what is called its reliability – do the items that make up an element actually all measure that same element? As part of the development of the EIQ, reliability measures were computed for each of the element scales and these were all found to be at an acceptable level. However, evidence for the validity of the EIQ is even more important. In answer to the question is EI relevant at work, we have recently shown that there does appear to be a relationship between EIQ scores and work performance. We took the EIQ scores of staff in managerial and sales positions and related them to job performance measures taken at the same point in time in a number of different companies.

Our study of Team Leaders in a pharmaceutical company provided an opportunity to investigate the validity of the EIQ: M as measures of current performance were available. The results provided clear evidence for the validity of the (self) EIQ: M. The total EIQ: M score was highly significantly related to the performance measures, as were six of the elements (all apart from Sensitivity). The results from the 360° version of EIQ: M provided further support. Once again, total score on EIQ: M 360° was significantly correlated with performance ratings. Focusing on the elements, Resilience and Motivation were significantly related to the performance measure, while Sensitivity (unlike the self reports), Influence and Intuitiveness were related to some aspects of the performance. In contrast to the self-assessments, Self-awareness and Conscientiousness were not significantly related to performance. However, of greater importance, when the results for the combined self and boss scores were combined, the results demonstrated the value of aggregating the scores from the two. The total EQ score was highly significantly related to all the performance measures, while on the specific elements six of the seven were significantly related to performance.

Two of the earliest studies to demonstrate the value of EI at work were on sales staff. In our own study of sales staff, self assessments showed that only Resilience and Motivation were related to job performance, but the 360° assessment by the boss showed that four elements and the overall EQ score were significantly correlated with job performance ratings provided by the boss's boss.

Another study of managers was one part of a much larger investigation into the quality of working life and stress of managers in a large multi-national retail organisation conducted by a colleague of ours, Mark Slaski. In addition to a number of measures of stress and job performance, participants completed the EIQ: M. Links were found between the EIQ scores and scores from two measures of morale and stress at work which demonstrated that EI is an important determinant of satisfaction and stress at work, the latter inversely related to EI. Significant relationships were also found between EIQ and current job performance, thus providing further evidence of the EIQ for predicting job performance. Finally, the results showed that EI scores improved after training, demonstrating that EI is capable of being developed.

An interesting study of call centre staff used the EIQ: G. Three organisations (two financial and one public sector) took part in this study. They provided demographic (age, gender and length of service) and performance data, provided by means of an individual performance assessment by the personnel department in the organisation. Overall emotional intelligence (as measured by the EIQ: G) was significantly related to centre agent performance, as were six of the seven elements. The exception, Intuitiveness, was related to performance, but negatively, i.e. poorer performers tended to get higher scores. In addition, a comparison between high and low performing groups showed all the EI elements (apart from Influence and Self-awareness) differentiated between the high and low performing groups of agents. When reviewing the biographical results, overall EIQ was not related to length of service.

Emotional Intelligence in the BT Global Challenge Round-the-World Yacht Race

We were fortunate to be invited to test all the crews in the BT Global Challenge Round-the-World Yacht Race during 2000/1. Twelve identical yachts, skippered by an elite group of yachtspeople, took part in the race. While the skippers were all experienced sailors, 70 per cent of the crew volunteers had never sailed before they were selected to take part in the most challenging amateur yacht race.

One aim of this study was to explore the relationship between the emotional intelligence of the skippers and crews, their team dynamics and overall race results. At the start of the race, data was collected on participants' emotional intelligence via the EIQ: M, competencies and personality questionnaires.

The focus of this research was to explore links between these personal and team characteristics and the boats' performance in the race. The main performance measure used was the official race result.

Analysing the make-up of the participants at the outset, we found that the 12 skippers as a group were highly emotionally intelligent. In contrast, the crew generally had lower levels of emotional intelligence, although they had higher levels in terms of Interpersonal Sensitivity and Conscientiousness.

A number of crew members dropped out during the course of the race for reasons other than health and we were curious to know if the personal characteristics of those who stayed differed from those of the people who left. Interestingly, those who stayed had higher overall levels of emotional intelligence, especially Conscientiousness, than those who left.

The emotional intelligence of skippers and the core crew was assessed both before and after the race. No action was taken to develop their emotional intelligence during the race. However, we found that, at the end of the race, the skippers' Intuitiveness had increased. For crews, the race appeared to have had the effect of reducing overall levels of emotional intelligence and, specifically, their Interpersonal Sensitivity and Influence. Nevertheless, when looking specifically at the more successful crews, their overall emotional intelligence had not declined while their Intuitiveness had actually increased (as with the skippers). We will return to this subject later.

The most interesting findings were from the overall race performance. Looking first at the skippers, we found that the successful ones tended to be more emotionally intelligent and in particular had higher Interpersonal Sensitivity. In contrast, the crew's results showed, somewhat unexpectedly, that the more successful boats tended to have crews with higher levels of reasoning ability and intellectual competencies (IQ rather than EQ). To explore the contribution of all key findings relating to performance, the total teamworking (Team Process) score for each boat was added to the two main personal qualities found to be significant, the skippers' Emotional

Intelligence (EQ) and the crews' Intellectual Competencies (IQ). These three variables accounted for just over one-half (51 per cent) of the total variation of the boats' race performance.

The results of our research show that as well as being important for successful performance at work, EI also appears to be an important ingredient for success as a skipper in a really demanding yacht race. In the next chapter we will explore in much greater detail the nature of the seven elements of emotional intelligence measured by the four versions of EIQ.

What is the Measure Telling Us?

In the previous chapter we described our research and the development of a measure of emotional intelligence. **Appendix I** provides a sample report on emotional intelligence which is generated from the instrument developed to measure it. In a managerial context (the EIQ: M) the report provides:

(a) a description of the individual's overall emotional intelligence;

(b) a description of their position on each of the seven scales described in the previous section. This examines the individual's strengths and development needs indicated by their score on the scale;

(c) general suggestions for areas that can be focused on when building and developing capability on each of the scales and hence the overall level of emotional intelligence.

This report is based on self-assessment. **Appendix II** shows a specimen report using the 360° version described in **chapter 3**. In addition to the information provided in the self-assessment, this version provides a picture of how others see an individual's emotional intelligence and how the comparisons can provide further development insights.

In this chapter we will use the format of the self-assessment report for exploring what the measure of emotional intelligence tells us about an individual's strengths, weaknesses and development needs. We will do this by working through the profiles of an above- and below-average scorer on the instrument and will focus on exploring what the profile of each of these 'hypothetical' individuals means. For ease of illustration we have referred to 'above average' as 'high' and 'below average' as 'low'. The profiles for these two individuals are shown in **Figures 4.1** and **4.2**. In addition, we will explore how the 360° report can add to the picture which emerges.

Figure 4.1: Emotional Intelligence Report – Profile Chart for Pat Low

Name: Pat Low

Sten	1	2	3	4	5	6	7	8	9	10	
A	1	.	.	.	.	.	.	.	.	.	Self-awareness
B	.	.	3	.	.	.	.	.	.	.	Emotional Resilience
C	.	.	3	.	.	.	.	.	.	.	Motivation
D	.	.	.	.	5	.	.	.	.	.	Interpersonal Sensitivity
E	.	.	3	.	.	.	.	.	.	.	Influence
F	.	.	.	.	5	.	.	.	.	.	Intuitiveness
G	.	.	.	.	.	.	7	.	.	.	Conscientiousness
EI	.	.	.	4	.	.	.	.	.	.	Overall EI
Percentile	1	4	11	23	40	60	77	89	96	99	

Norms used: International Management Sample

Figure 4.2: Emotional Intelligence Report – Profile Chart for Sam High

Name: Sam High

Sten	1	2	3	4	5	6	7	8	9	10	
A	.	.	.	.	.	.	7	.	.	.	Self-awareness
B	.	.	.	.	.	.	.	.	9	.	Emotional Resilience
C	.	.	.	.	.	.	7	.	.	.	Motivation
D	.	.	.	.	.	.	.	.	9	.	Interpersonal Sensitivity
E	.	.	.	.	.	.	7	.	.	.	Influence
F	.	.	.	.	.	.	.	8	.	.	Intuitiveness
G	.	.	.	.	.	.	.	.	9	.	Conscientiousness
EI	.	.	.	.	.	.	.	8	.	.	Overall EI
Percentile	1	4	11	23	40	60	77	89	96	99	

Norms used: International Management Sample

Overall Emotional Intelligence

This section examines the overall profile of the individual on a ten-point scale.

Pat Low

On this overall scale Pat has scored four which indicates that his level of emotional intelligence is below the average range. This implies that he has a restricted understanding of his feelings and how they impact on his actions and decisions. He could benefit from becoming somewhat more reflective in his decision-making and should try to recognise the importance of his feelings in this process.

A barrier on relying on his feelings in work-related decisions may be his tendency to feel somewhat 'swamped' by feelings and emotions. He would benefit by being able to acknowledge these, and to manage them effectively in pursuing work-related goals. Indeed, this mind-set may help him to feel less personally affronted by rejection of his ideas or proposals.

The profile of the seven elements indicates that Pat may feel uncomfortable in making difficult decisions and may tend to seek certainty based on analytical or objective reasoning. This could delay decision-making, or attempting to enforce high degrees of formalisation on processes. In difficult situations this tendency can lead to high levels of personal stress which he may attempt to offset by focusing on controls or mechanisms for depersonalising the process of arriving at decisions.

When working with groups Pat will tend to attempt to avoid conflict, which he dislikes. He may attempt to minimise conflict by focusing on objective or fact-based processes. In broad terms he finds that focusing on process and objectivity avoids interpersonal reliance on the building and exercise of trust.

When working with others, Pat's communication style tends to be unduly formal and based on fact rather than his emotions and feelings.

When working with individuals and groups Pat could benefit from listening carefully to others' viewpoints, reflecting on their own needs and recognising their emotions and concerns.

Sam High

On the overall scale Sam has scored eight which indicates that she has a clear understanding of her own feelings and is able to take them into account when making decisions with confidence. While aware of her own moods she has a high focus on required outcomes and is able to work to achieve results in spite of personal moods. When interacting with others, Sam is able to express her feelings clearly without causing problems.

Overall, she would appear to be highly self-motivated and able to take a long-term perspective. While feeling under pressure at times, Sam is able to use anxiety to perform well. Her clear view of longer-term goals, and commitment to these, helps to maintain actions in the face of setbacks and difficulties. When interacting with others she has a well-developed sense of their feelings, but uses this constructively to ensure that conflict is surfaced and handled effectively. In working with a group Sam is able to sense the pulse of relationships effectively and ensure that unstated feelings and emotions are brought to the surface. In general she will tend to take a leadership role which, because of her approach, will be appreciated by the group. Sam's approach to dealing with others, in a work context, will be characterised by high levels of trust and an ability to balance compassion and caring with focus on goal achievement.

In general she tends to have an open communication style and listens actively to others. While maintaining such a style she is able to ensure that she is direct in expressing her own views and opinions.

In making decisions Sam is effective and comfortable in balancing both 'hard' and 'soft' issues and considerations. She tends to accept personal responsibility for decisions, but does not find this stressful and thus does not have a high need for structure and control in managing her working relationships with others.

While this provides an overall picture, the detailed meaning of the profile is explored through examination of the seven scales. This is illustrated below.

Self-awareness

Pat Low

On this ten-point scale Pat achieved a score of one. This indicates that Pat would benefit from reflecting on specific incidents or situations and identifying opportunities to intervene in a way which gives him greater control and an opportunity to act in a way which is independent of his initial feeling of 'helplessness' or inability to manage his feelings.

While Pat's overall result is below the average range on self-awareness, he might wish to exploit his strengths in controlling his mood; recognising them and making specific attempts to change them and understanding and controlling his feelings.

Sam High

On the self-awareness scale Sam scores seven. This suggests that Sam is highly aware of her feelings in a range of work-related situations. Sam should reflect on her abilities to manage a range of situations and become more conscious of the way in which this awareness is interpreted and applied in practical behaviours. This surfacing and reinforcing of awareness will enable her to employ the behaviours productively in a consistent manner.

Emotional Resilience

Pat Low

On this ten-point scale, Pat scores three, which would suggest that he tends to be frustrated by criticism or challenge. Pat needs to find a way of depersonalising such reactions and to try to see challenge as an opportunity to engage others in building a robust solution to a difficult problem.

While Pat's overall result is below the average range on emotional resilience, he might wish to exploit his strengths in relation to: maintaining performance when under pressure; adapting his behaviour to different situations; adapting his behaviour based on his understanding of the views of those he is dealing with; making every effort to maintain effectiveness in the face of insults; and becoming effective in a wide range of different situations.

Sam High

Sam scores nine on this scale, which indicates that she has a high level of emotional resilience. This is evident by her ability to adapt to a range of situations and to tolerate ambiguity and challenge. She should reflect on the behaviours she exhibits in such diverse situations and ensure that these are incorporated into a broad range of behaviours.

Motivation

Pat Low

On this scale Pat scores three which indicates that he tends to be averse to demonstrating motivation to a goal or course of action. Pat can enhance his performance by finding a basis for achieving alignment between personal and organisational goals, thus building a personal commitment to them.

While the overall result is below the average range on motivation, Pat might wish to exploit his strengths in setting high, stretching goals for himself when contributing to projects and tasks.

Sam High

Sam scores seven in this scale which indicates a tendency to be very focused on results or outcomes. Sam tends to exhibit high levels of commitment and focus, and would benefit from developing a deeper understanding of the source of her personal motivation, and consequently extending this across a wider range of situations.

Interpersonal Sensitivity

Pat Low

This is an area in which Pat tends to be closer to an average score (five). The score indicates that Pat tends to be aware that in some previous situations he has clearly involved others in problem solving and decision-making. However, Pat may feel frustrated that he cannot consistently achieve high levels of engagement and commitment. He should reflect on the behaviours which he exhibited in successful situations and attempt to replicate these across a wider range of situations.

Sam High

On this scale Sam scores very highly (nine). This indicates that Sam tends to recognise the need to engage others in problem-solving and decision-making while recognising the uncertainties of others and their need to have these addressed. Sam tends to focus on results and may be less concerned with how these are achieved. She needs to recognise the behaviours which build this understanding and 'buy-in' and try to extend these across a wider range of situations and problems.

Influence

Pat Low

On this scale Pat scores three which suggests that he may sometimes find it difficult to win others over to his point of view. Pat should develop his ability to present a viewpoint which takes account of alternative perspectives and which taps into the emotions, motives and drives of others.

Sam High

Sam scores seven which indicates that she can be effective in persuading others to adopt her interpretation of a situation or need for action. Sam should reflect on specific behaviours which elicit such a response and develop strategies to incorporate these behaviours into all of her interactions.

Intuitiveness

Pat Low

Although low on the overall EI score, this scale is in the average range which indicates that Pat is probably good at balancing the needs of both the situation and of others to get a clear decision in various difficult situations. He needs to ensure that others understand the situation being discussed and that he communicates the complexity of business decisions. He needs to develop an ability to understand and communicate the risks associated with both making and delaying decisions. Pat also needs to recognise that, in the face of incomplete information, intuition (based on experience) may be a valid input to the decision.

Sam High

On this scale Sam scored eight which means that she is able to make decisions in difficult situations and cope with incomplete or ambiguous information. Sam should focus on reinforcing the behaviours which ensure others 'buy-in' to such decisions and try to understand which behaviours help to build decision support.

Conscientiousness

Pat Low

Although low on the overall EI score, this is Pat's highest scale score which means he is an individual whose words and actions are consistent. Pat demonstrates a high degree of personal commitment to both goals and behaviours. He needs to recognise the impact of such congruent behaviour and ensure that this is generalised across a wide range of challenges and situations. In his behaviour and personal conduct, he usually demonstrates high ethical standards. Generally, Pat is able to achieve results without engaging in expedient behaviour.

Sam High

Sam scores nine on this scale which means she usually behaves in a way that her words and actions are consistent. She demonstrates a high degree of personal commitment to both goals and behaviours and needs to recognise the impact of such congruent behaviour and ensure that this is generalised across a wide range of challenges and situations. In Sam's own personal conduct she demonstrates high ethical standards. Generally, Sam is able to achieve excellent results without engaging in expedient behaviour.

In this last element, both Sam and Pat are similar, although their overall profiles are significantly different.

Reviewing the high and low profiles above, hopefully, provides greater insight into what is being uncovered by the measure of emotional intelligence. From this the meaning of the overall score becomes less significant than developing an understanding of the individual components of emotional intelligence. Indeed the overall measure may be seen to reflect the degree to which the individual is able to balance the apparently contradictory elements of emotional intelligence. For example, a high overall score would indicate a high degree of motivation **and** a high level of conscientiousness. These are elements of an individual's make-up which are often viewed as alternatives (e.g. high motivation, low conscientiousness) rather than moving together. The overall score may be a reflection of an individual's ability to manage apparently competing personal drives and behaviours. This is an issue which we return to in **chapter 5**.

Both reports presented so far represent those generated from self-assessment questionnaires. However, as suggested earlier, additional value is provided by means of reviewing self-assessment alongside the feedback provided by others by means of the 360° report. **Figures 4.3** and **4.4** show Sam High's self-assessment report and the 360° reports compared with each other.

Figure 4.3: Emotional Intelligence Report – Sam High

(a) Self-assessment

Sten	1	2	3	4	5	6	7	8	9	10	
A	.	.	.	.	.	.	7	.	.	.	Self-awareness
B	.	.	.	.	.	.	.	.	9	.	Emotional Resilience
C	.	.	.	.	.	.	7	.	.	.	Motivation
D	.	.	.	.	.	.	.	.	9	.	Interpersonal Sensitivity
E	.	.	.	.	.	.	7	.	.	.	Influence
F	.	.	.	.	.	.	.	8	.	.	Intuitiveness
G	.	.	.	.	.	.	.	.	9	.	Conscientiousness
EI	.	.	.	.	.	.	.	8	.	.	Overall EI
Percentile	1	4	11	23	40	60	77	89	96	99	

Norms used: International Management Sample

Figure 4.4: Emotional Intelligence Report – Sam High

(b) Colleagues

Sten	1	2	3	4	5	6	7	8	9	10	
A	.	.	.	.	.	6	.	.	.	.	Self-awareness
B	.	.	.	.	.	.	.	.	.	10	Emotional Resilience
C	.	.	.	.	.	.	.	.	9	.	Motivation
D	.	.	.	.	.	.	7	.	.	.	Interpersonal Sensitivity
E	.	.	.	.	5	.	.	.	.	.	Influence
F	.	.	.	.	.	6	.	.	.	.	Intuitiveness
G	.	.	.	.	.	.	.	8	.	.	Conscientiousness
EI	.	.	.	.	.	.	.	.	9	.	Overall EI
Percentile	1	4	11	23	40	60	77	89	96	99	

Norms used: International Management Sample

When interpreting this result it is evident that the overall profiles are relatively close. However, in analysing the feedback it is helpful to reflect on the similarities and differences between the self-assessment and the assessment provided by colleagues. When reviewing these differences it is important to recognise that the self-assessment may differ from that of colleagues because of differences in perception. It could prove valuable for Sam High to explore these differences by seeking the opportunity to learn and develop, rather than by becoming overly concerned with the correctness (in an absolute sense) of either assessment. For example, if she has a more positive overall view of her emotional intelligence, it may be more useful if she tries to understand the reasons for the difference, rather than trying to identify which view is 'correct'.

Having looked at the overall picture, it could be helpful to review the individual scales to identify which aspects of emotional intelligence show the greatest differences in perception. If the differences in ratings are notable, this may indicate a need to focus carefully on the elements of difference.

In the case of Sam High, the major areas of difference to explore would appear to be Interpersonal Sensitivity, Influence and Motivation. The detailed report (see **Appendix II**) provides further information in terms of the range of responses provided. Using the overall differences and range data Sam High could consider approaches to deepening her understanding and building a development plan. These could include:

- reflecting on the reasons why differences may have arisen;

- considering the range of colleagues she asked for feedback and reflecting on how well they know her in a work context;

- meeting with individuals who provided feedback and sharing her overall results with an aim to understand (in a non-judgemental way) the differences; and

- discussing with others (including those who provided feedback) her proposed development actions and seeking their reactions and feedback.

Conclusion

In this chapter we have illustrated what a measure of emotional intelligence may mean for an individual. The nature of the measure and its broader interpretation is explored further in the next chapter.

Towards a Model of Emotional Intelligence

Introduction

By now you should have a much clearer picture of what emotional intelligence is and how it can be measured. It should also be evident that emotional intelligence accounts for a lot of the variation in individual success in terms of making long term progress at work.

Two further and important issues arise at this point.

- The relationship between emotional intelligence and job performance
- The development of emotional intelligence.

To address these two issues it is important to reflect on how emotional intelligence relates to aspects of performance and development at work. While **chapter 7** explores the development question in more detail, this chapter is designed to explore how emotional intelligence relates to other drivers of performance and builds a model which is intended to place emotional intelligence in a broader context.

The Link between EI and Performance

Early writing on emotional intelligence focused on the 'success' of individuals in their chosen career or profession. In Daniel Goleman's original book he provided a few examples of organisationally-based studies which demonstrated a link between emotional intelligence and performance. The most direct links had been provided by a small number of studies which had examined relationships between emotional intelligence and the performance of sales staff in financial services organisations. These had tended to show a positive relationship between the two.

In a very different type of study two researchers (Kelley and Caplan) conducted research at the Research and Development Centre for the Bell Telephone Company. They were interested in finding out what it took to be seen as a 'star' performer among a bright and talented group of researchers in the laboratory. Those rated as 'stars' had many of the components of high emotional intelligence. Two studies of sales staff by Martinez and Gordon also showed a link between EI and sales performance.

When we first reviewed the literature, these were the only studies we could find which had been conducted within companies. We concluded that this was an important area to address and so focused on our own research on the possible links between EI and performance at work. As we showed in **chapter 3**, we have now found that EI is indeed related to performance in a number of jobs:

- Managers
- Team leaders
- Sales staff
- Call centre staff

In addition, we have found that EI is important outside the work situation, for example, the skippers of yachts in a nine-month race around the world.

Furthermore, the evidence linking emotional intelligence to success (in terms of progression in the organisation) provides an indirect link to performance. This line of argument is developed on the premise that, in most situations, an individual is unlikely to be able to progress within an organisation without a track record of successful performance. There is indeed nothing particularly new in relating track record to success in an organisation. In many situations there is a clear 'value tree' which can be identified linking the components of individuals, their performance and their success. This relationship is shown diagrammatically in **Figure 5.1.**

Figure 5.1: Success and the Individual

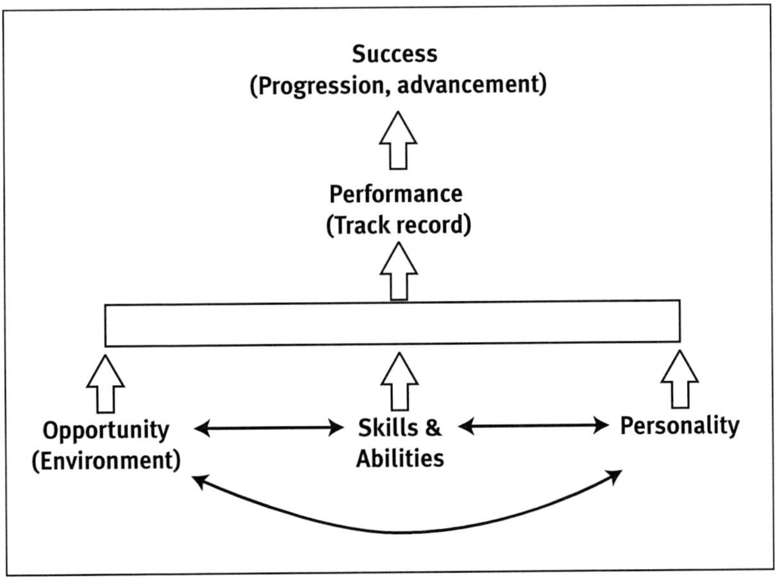

Much of the research and literature on identification of potential and exploration of performance has touched on the building blocks of personality, skills and abilities and environment as well as their interrelationships. In looking at emotional intelligence in this way the 'traditional' viewpoint is maintained. Within these three building blocks, the issue of environment is perhaps the broadest and, ultimately, the most difficult to pin down. This takes us into the realms of organisational values and corporate culture. However, even though this is a difficult area it does need to be explored and we will return to this in more detail in **chapter 10**. The other two building blocks (skills and personality) are often linked in the discussion and definition of competencies.

The emerging view that a number of competency frameworks contain a significant number of competencies which are similar to components of emotional intelligence can be taken as further indication of potential performance linkages. The main thrust of much of the competency-based research over the last decade or so has been the examination of competencies in relation to the delivery of superior performance. Indeed many competency frameworks are rooted in research designed to isolate the traits, motivations and behaviours associated with superior performance. In Daniel Goleman's book on working with emotional intelligence (1998) he specifically examines the parallels between emotional intelligence and the McBer consultancy's database to illustrate the linkages between emotional intelligence and performance.

When discussing performance evidence and linkages it is inevitable that questions will arise in terms of defining how performance should be measured. This is the focus of much heated and exhaustive debate among both practitioners and academics in relation to many aspects of individual and organisational behaviour. As a topic it warrants a book in its own right (and indeed has been examined many times). It is not our intention to engage in this debate in this book, but it is worth mentioning that there is an emerging consensus that, in looking at individual and organisational performance, there is a need to consider both 'hard' and 'soft' measures of performance. Specific results (often financial) should be considered alongside measures or indicators of less tangible outcomes such as staff morale or customer satisfaction. In organisational terms we are seeing this shift in terms of greater use of the 'Balanced Business Scorecard' (or similar multiple performance measures), a means of measuring performance in terms of more than just financial data (e.g. including measures of customer and employee satisfaction). At the individual level we are seeing the growth in the use of 360° (or multiple source) feedback as an element in performance appraisal systems to complement assessment of more 'traditional' measures such as goals, objectives and targets.

One way of looking at the growing use of 'hard' and 'soft' measures in combination is that the specific outcome measures (the 'hard' measures) give indications of the achievement of relatively short-term performance goals, while the measures relating to employee and customer satisfaction (the 'soft' measures) relate to the creation of foundations for future performance. This can be highly significant to organisations which believe that it is the people within the organisation who provide the basis for sustainable and long-term competitive advantage.

When performance is viewed in this light, the links between emotional intelligence and performance are relatively self-evident (although further research to demonstrate empirically the linkage remains both valuable and important). The links appear increasingly important when looking at individuals in leadership positions (a topic which is explored in more detail in **chapter 8**).

How Might the Linkage Work?

In **chapter 2**, we emphasised the significance of 'balance' in emotional intelligence. At its basic level it can be seen as the ability to balance 'hard' and 'soft' elements when arriving at business decisions. This was captured in the phrase 'tough love' – the ability to care about individuals and be aware of and sensitive to their needs, while also driving forward to achieve necessary (and often challenging) business goals. This concept of balance applies to many of the elements of emotional intelligence and was summarised in **Figure 2.2** in **chapter 2**. Indeed, within a number of discussions about emotional intelligence, the idea of balance between groups of elements is raised. For example the Bar-on Emotional Intelligence Test identifies the following broad (and potentially conflicting) categories:

Intrapersonal: aspects concerned with the nature of the individual and their self-image.

Interpersonal: those elements concerned with the interaction of the individual with others.

Stress Management: ability to deal with the impact of pressures, conflicting demands and pressures on self-image and values in a way which is not damaging to the individual.

Mood: aspects relating to transient states of mind and the ability to cope with these (e.g. optimism, happiness, disappointment).

The concept of balance is by no means new to psychology. The summary of the Bar-on model (above) can be seen as relating to the challenges faced by many individuals within their daily lives; challenges addressed many years ago by leading psychologists such as Freud and Jung. The issues associated with balancing conflicting aspects of oneself lies at the heart of Freudian psychology. The translation of this particular viewpoint into an accessible model with practical individual and organisational applications was achieved most notably through the development of 'transactional analysis' by Eric Berne (and widely popularised in the book *I'm OK; You're OK* by Thomas Harris). This framework explores interactions between people based on their use of parent, child or adult ego states. It identifies that the most effective interactions occur when both participants are using the adult ego state. Indeed a number of researchers and authors working in the field of emotional intelligence have acknowledged the influence on their work of the 'transactional analysis' models and applications.

To an extent, the model proposed in **chapter 2** may be seen to have links to the Freudian concepts of Id, Ego and Superego, with the drivers being the Id, the Enablers the Ego and the constrainers the Superego. It may be seen to be following much that has been written about personality and behaviour at work. A review of the vast literature associated with this would point to these groupings. The three groupings can be seen to contain elements which relate to personality, attitudes, values, beliefs, experience, skills and abilities.

However, the mix of these elements vary in their likely impact on the overall component. This may be seen from the following:

- Drivers: motivation, personality, attitudes, values and beliefs
- Constrainers: experience, personality, confidence, self-belief, self-image, abilities
- Enablers: skills, competencies, environment

A Model of Emotional Intelligence

When reflecting on the link between EI and performance, making a distinction between Inter- and Intra-Personal elements/components is important, especially for research into managerial performance because Inter-personal elements are paramount if managers are to achieve results with or through colleagues. This distinction can be superimposed on the basic EI model above and is presented in **Table 5.1**. This model clearly differentiates between Inter- and Intra-Personal elements and also reflects the importance of the Inter-Personal Enablers to the link with performance, the other five elements being channelled through these two.

Table 5.1: EI Model and Associated Elements

Model Components	EI Elements
Driver	Motivation
Constrainer	Conscientiousness
Intra-Personal Enablers	Self-awareness Emotional Resilience Intuitiveness
Inter-Personal Enablers	Interpersonal Sensitivity Influence

The relationship between the model in **chapter 2** and this broader discussion can be further illuminated by reviewing what we found when comparing our emotional intelligence factors with elements of other personality tests (e.g. the 16PF and OPQ). These are summarised in **Table 5.2**. Reviewing this table highlights the challenge of balancing potentially contradictory elements of oneself, which appears to be at the heart of emotional intelligence.

Table 5.2: EI Model and Personality Factors & Personal Competencies

Model Components	EI Elements	Personality Factors & Competencies
Driver	Motivation	Energy Achievement Motivation Motivating Others
Constrainer	Conscientiousness	Controlled High Self-Confidence
Personal Enablers	Self-Awareness Emotional Resilience Intuitiveness	Low Assertiveness Low Independence High Superego Strength Toughness Well-adjusted Low Control Independence
Inter-Personal Enablers	Influence Sensitivity	Persuasiveness Sensitivity Stress Tolerance Low Assertiveness Low Independence

Building a Bigger Picture

When examining the components of emotional intelligence and their links with performance and success, it is clear from the above that the picture is somewhat complex. In the original work on emotional intelligence and Goleman's summary of this, it is evident that IQ (as traditionally measured) needs to be brought into account. Indeed this assertion is borne out not only by general research into IQ and performance, but also by the authors' research into emotional intelligence. Emotional intelligence is not only about balancing the diverse, and often conflicting, elements associated with the concept, but also balancing all of these with the rational components of work and decision-making which require the application of more traditional IQ-related attributes.

In the seven-year follow-up study of 100 general managers, the authors ascertained that a set of managerial competencies which were different from both emotional intelligence and intellectual competencies (IQ) played a significant part in explaining variations in individual success in terms of advancement within an organisation. Indeed they found that a combination of IQ, emotional intelligence (EQ) and a set of managerial competencies (labelled as MQ) accounted for over 70 per cent of variations in individual success (in terms of advancement within their organisation). Building from these findings leads to the development of a model that places emotional intelligence in a pivotal position when balancing elements of the make-up of an individual and assisting in the achievement of superior performance.

This model should also reflect the importance of intellectual competencies (IQ) and managerial competencies (MQ). In our general managers' study, we showed that the IQ competencies cover four broad categories – Analysis & Judgement; Planning & Organising; Perspective and Risk-taking & Creativity – which all appear to constitute Intra-Personal qualities. In contrast, the MQ competencies – Supervising Others; Communicating and Achieving Results – are all clearly Inter-Personal qualities.

Figure 5.2: A Model of Emotional Intelligence including IQ and
MQ Competencies

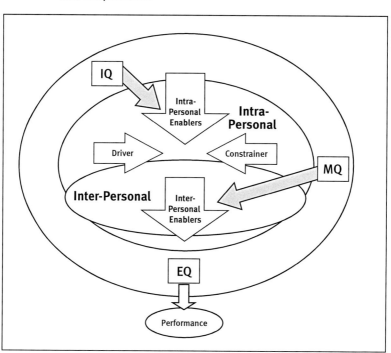

A model which captures *all* of these relationships is presented in **Figure 5.2.**
The proposition implied in this model is that emotional intelligence
represents the overall ability to pull together a wide range of an individual's
personality characteristics and skills to deliver superior performance. The
possession of an average-to-above-average IQ and reasonably developed
managerial competencies may be viewed as the 'needed to play' components
of organisational success, and these, together with well-developed
emotional intelligence, represent the 'needed to win' components of success.

Testing the Model in Practice

The revised model was tested using the data from three of the studies
reported in **chapter 3** and this analysis facilitated our understanding of the

development of EI. We tested different combinations of Inter- and Intra-personal elements of EI, IQ and MQ competencies and found support from the Team Leaders and Retail Managers studies for the following propositions:

- *Multiplacative Relationship* – A Multiple of Inter-Personal *times* Personal elements scores will be significantly related to performance.

- *Additive Relationship* – Inter-Personal *plus* Personal elements scores will be significantly related to performance.

- *Multiplacative Relationship* with *Conscientiousness* scored negatively – Inter-Personal minus Conscientiousness, a Constrainer, *plus* IQ times Personal elements *plus* MQ will be significantly related to performance.

- *Additive Relationship* with *Conscientiousness* scored negatively – Inter-Personal minus Conscientiousness, a Constrainer, *plus* IQ *plus* Personal elements plus MQ will be significantly related to performance.

For the first time, to our knowledge, a model to explain the complex inter-relationships between elements of emotional intelligence has been supported by hard evidence from the business world.

Our model therefore appears to represent a reasonable framework for explaining and developing the ideas summarised in **Figure 5.2**. However, the impact of the environment or organisational culture is not accounted for by the model shown in this figure. In spite of what we read about emotional intelligence, there are a significant number of very 'successful' people who do not overtly display many of the characteristics that we have described so far. Does this, therefore, mean that our assertions are flawed? Indeed it could. However, we believe that there is a more powerful alternative explanation. From our experience (and from the literature) it is evident that the culture or climate within an organisation has a significant impact on decisions around promotions and perceptions of success and failure. In an organisation which has a culture of only valuing and rewarding the achievement of short-term financial gains it is unlikely that individuals who are emotionally intelligent will progress. It is also unlikely that much effort will be placed in developing such abilities. Even if an organisation attracts such individuals they are unlikely to find much fulfilment in working for it and will leave. This means that the culture feeds on its own experience and reinforces the clinical results-only culture. It becomes a place in which 'managers are rewarded for succeeding badly'. In the view of many experts this is not the basis for long-term sustainable corporate success, but in the experience of many it is a current reality. Thus, if we want to be able to fully understand the significance of emotional intelligence we need to recognise that the relationship between EI and performance is mediated by corporate culture. This leads to our overall model which is shown in **Figure 5.3**.

Figure 5.3: A Model of Emotional Intelligence in Context including Organisation Culture

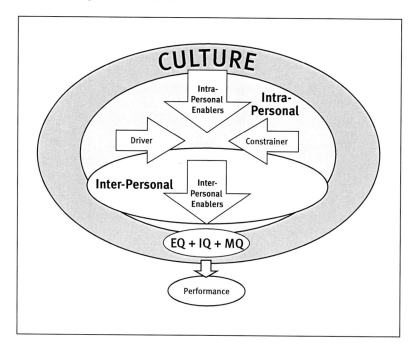

Conclusion

Our overall model, and the ideas explored in this chapter, will help us to formulate ideas on how emotional intelligence may be developed. However, they also point to a need to explore the impact of corporate culture on what needs to happen beyond the level of individual development in order to realise the potential offered by an understanding of the nature and benefits of emotional intelligence. This we shall do in **chapter 10**.

What is My Emotional Intelligence?

Introduction

Having built a case for the value of emotional intelligence in contributing to success at work, it is inevitable that anyone reading this would be interested in working out their own level of emotional intelligence. Hopefully, such an interested reader would recognise that this question cannot be answered by a *simple* self-administered questionnaire. Emotional intelligence is a wide-ranging and complex concept with no quick or easy indicators. The level of an individual's emotional intelligence may be assessed through a structured examination of a specific group of competencies or through using a well-researched and developed psychometric assessment. Many readers may find this frustrating as they will want to know their own level of emotional intelligence so that they can take action to develop and improve their capability in this area. This brief chapter has been developed to help the reader conduct a tentative assessment of their emotional intelligence to satisfy their curiosity and help them approach the balance of the book with a number of practical questions in mind. These can be explored further when reading **chapter 7**, Can Emotional Intelligence be Developed? Should the reader require a more specific assessment before reflecting on developmental activity we have proposed a process for building a firmer foundation for their assessment. Those who seek an absolute measure of their emotional intelligence should arrange to take the full psychometric assessment.

Making an Initial Assessment

A relatively straightforward way of making an initial assessment of your own level of emotional intelligence is to reflect on the definitions of the seven component elements described in **chapter 3**. For each of these elements we have outlined below how you might feel or behave if you have particularly high or low levels of the element within your current repertoire of behaviours.

Self-awareness

High Level

- Aware of your feelings and emotions in a wide range of situations.

- If you become aware of feelings or moods which disrupt your performance you attempt to control or manage them and believe it is possible to do this.

- In general you have a positive outlook on life.

Low Level

- You tend not to spend time reflecting on your feelings and are generally unaware of them in a work context.

- Overall you do not believe it is feasible to manage your feelings.

Emotional Resilience

High Level

- You find it relatively easy to adjust to new situations or circumstances while at the same time focusing on your overall performance.

- In general you do not find it difficult to balance the need to get a job done with the needs and concerns of those who you have to persuade to help you.

Low Level

- If you are faced with personal criticism or challenge you tend to find that your performance suffers.

- You find it difficult to deliver consistent performance across a range of situations.

- In the face of criticism or rejection you can continue to focus on a task or your overall goals and aspirations.

- When under pressure you can become irritable or volatile.

Motivation

High Level

- You know that you are consistently focused on results and work to overcome problems in ensuring that you attain your goals.

- You tend to set yourself challenging goals.

- You tend to set, or encourage others who work for you to set, challenging goals.

- You are able to achieve high levels of performance in a variety of situations.

- You believe that the potential of individuals far exceeds what is normally sought or expected in terms of contribution.

Low Level

- You dislike committing to goals for yourself.

- You are unwilling or unable to encourage others to commit to challenging goals.

- You are willing to accept barriers to achieving goals without spending time and effort to challenge these barriers.

- You do not believe that either yourself or others working with you can achieve truly stretching objectives.

Interpersonal Sensitivity

High Level

- You invest time and effort in clarifying and discussing issues with others.

- You are willing to accept the views of others or their explanations or interpretations of situations.

- You are willing to lay aside your own preferred solution when presented with a clearly better one.

- You are careful in listening to others and always check that you have understood them.

- You involve those who work for you in setting goals and objectives.

Low Level

- You impose goals and objectives on others.

- Even when discussing an issue or topic you tend to ensure that your view prevails.

- You are conscious of your hierarchical relationship with others and exploit this to achieve goals you wish to achieve.

Influence

High Level

- You are effective in persuading others to accept your viewpoint on problems or issues.

- In listening to others you are able to use their needs or concerns as a vehicle for changing their behaviour.

- You are successful in getting others to change their perception of a problem or situation.

- You find it relatively easy to develop rapport with others.

Low Level

- You find it difficult to persuade others to accept and 'buy-in' to your ideas.

- You find that your perception of a situation and that of others rarely move closer together.

- You do not find it easy to develop rapport with others.

Intuitiveness

High Level

- You are consistently able to make decisions in difficult situations and build support for these decisions.

- You recognise that, in many situations, it is more important to make a decision and implement it than to have all possible information available.

- You understand the complexity of business decisions and are comfortable with balancing intuitive judgement and detailed analysis.

Low Level

- You are uncomfortable in making decisions unless you are certain that you have considered all angles and obtained all relevant information.

- You dislike ambiguous situations.

- You have few problems in delaying or postponing a decision until all information is available.

Conscientiousness

High Level

- You tend to demonstrate a high level of commitment to agreed goals and methods of working.

- You invest personal time and effort in ensuring that what you say and what you do are the same.

- You set and adhere to high personal standards of conduct.

Low Level

- You are willing to compromise on your values to achieve a goal.

- There are gaps between what you say and what you do.

- If you underperform you often believe it to be due to circumstances beyond your control and accept such performance.

Reflect on these elements and consider the extent to which you **consistently** exhibit behaviours at the high or low end of the scales. In making this judgement you may want to use the following assessment scale:

1. Consistently exhibit behaviours described as low level.

2. ...

3. Exhibit behaviours which consistently lie between the high and low level or find that they vary between high and low level behaviours.

4. ...

5. Consistently exhibit the behaviours described as high level.

Within this scale you can use points 2 and 4 to 'fine tune' your assessment. You could summarise your 'profile' in the format shown in **Table 6.1**.

Table 6.1: Initial Self-assessment

Scale	Low 1	2	Medium 3	4	High 5
Self-awareness					
Emotional Resilience					
Motivation					
Interpersonal Sensitivity					
Influence					
Intuitiveness					
Conscientiousness					
OVERALL					

Having scored yourself on the individual scales you can then decide where you might position yourself on the overall scale. For example, if all of your ratings are medium or below, you are likely to be medium or below on the overall scale. If all ratings are medium to high then your overall rating is likely to be within this range. If your own assessments are somewhat mixed (some high or low) your overall assessment should be around the medium level.

In looking at this initial assessment and how it is made up, it becomes clear that an overall rating of emotional intelligence in itself does not help with planning future development. While the overall EI level is a predictor of success, it is understanding the component parts which helps with planning development. Development of these elements can impact on the overall scale and thus influence future potential to succeed. Approaches to developing the elements of emotional intelligence are explored in more detail in **chapter 7**.

Refining the Assessment

The process outlined above provides a 'rough and ready' assessment of your current level and profile of emotional intelligence. If you have been completely honest when making such an assessment then it can be a helpful starting point in building your capabilities in this important area. However, finding out how others see you can prove to be even more valuable in establishing the 'base line' for future development. There is a lot of value in asking others to provide you with feedback on the same basis as you used in your initial self-assessment. Using the descriptions outlined above you can ask work colleagues (your boss, peers, etc.) to give their assessment. This can be a difficult process for them, so you might like to begin by asking an individual you work with and know well to start. If there is a lot of openness, trust and confidence between you, then the assessment process can be followed by a detailed discussion which can prove to be illuminating.

Getting feedback from one individual and contrasting the two perceptions (yours and theirs) can be very helpful. Getting input from a range of people who may have worked with you in differing situations and relationships is even more valuable. Analysis of a range of viewpoints will give you a much clearer picture of your overall level of emotional intelligence and identify any potential areas for action.

Although the discussions with individual 'raters' can be extremely valuable, an overall 'map' of perceptions can be even more helpful. **Table 6.2** illustrates the possible format of such a map.

Table 6.2: Assessment 'Map'

Scale	Own Rating	1	2	3	4	Average of Others
Self-awareness	3	4	3	3	3	3.25
Emotional Resilience	4	5	2	2	3	4.0
Motivation	5	5	4	2	3	3.5
Interpersonal Sensitivity	4	5	4	4	3	4.0
Influence	4	3	3	2	2	2.5
Intuitiveness	3	4	2	2	3	2.75
Conscientiousness	3	5	4	4	2	3.75
OVERALL	3.7	4.4	3.1	2.7	2.7	3.4

This 'map' will help you to build a picture of your development needs as it will raise a number of questions. Using **Table 6.2,** some of these might be:

- What makes rater 1 so consistently positive?

- Rater 2 seems closest to my own ratings. Why?

- I seem to be more positive about my own ratings than those who gave me feedback. Why? Does it mean that I don't really understand myself or that my colleagues misinterpret my actions in a way which differs from my intentions?

- Why do I see myself as being lower on conscientiousness than others do? Could this relate to a mismatch between my intentions and others' perceptions or a lack of clarity over my own values and beliefs?

- Although overall, those who have rated me appear to agree with my own rating, there are significant differences between myself and raters 2 and 3. Why?

A major step in understanding your development needs would be to spend time with each 'rater' discussing the differences in perception and understanding the types of behaviour which they would associate with higher level scores.

It is important to bear in mind that an exercise of this nature is not one relating to debate around the precision of assessment or measurement – it is focused on an interactive process of trying to understand, in broad terms, where you stand now in terms of emotional intelligence, and how you can improve your abilities in this significant area.

Broadening the Assessment

Throughout this book the focus has been on emotional intelligence in a work or business context. To build a broader picture of perceptions of your current level of emotional intelligence you might find it useful to get those who know you outside work to rate you on the scales we have already used. It can be illuminating to contrast work-based ratings with domestic/social-based ratings in order to build an understanding of your development needs.

Conclusion

This brief chapter has been designed to help the reader to identify where they are at the moment in terms of emotional intelligence and hence their main development needs. It is important to state that this approach has to be treated as tentative. It is based on broad scales and the acquisition of feedback from others on these broad scales. A more structured assessment should be undertaken by those who are seriously concerned as to their current actual level of emotional intelligence and more precise development needs.

Whether having undertaken a detailed assessment from the psychometric test (EIQ) or using the 'rough and ready' assessment outlined in this chapter, the reader should now be in a position where he/she knows where they are, in terms of emotional intelligence, and the major gaps they need to address. **Chapter 7** focuses on how to approach development activities designed to build capability (or exploit potential) on each of the seven dimensions of emotional intelligence which we have identified. However, an in-depth assessment of this complex area provides one with much greater confidence that the development is appropriately targeted.

Can Emotional Intelligence be Developed?

Introduction

In chapters 5 and **6** we introduced an overall model examining the components of emotional intelligence and their potential contribution to performance in a work context. In addition the opportunity was provided for readers to make an initial assessment of their own current level of emotional intelligence. This chapter considers the feasibility of an individual being able to develop their level of emotional intelligence and potential ways of doing this.

If, as research and assertions propose, emotional intelligence is a significant differentiator (given broadly equivalent levels of IQ) in terms of 'life success' and ultimately corporate success, then the question arises as to whether emotional intelligence can be developed or is it a more enduring personality trait? To an extent, this question invites a review of the elusive 'nature/nurture' argument, but this chapter is not setting out to revisit or resolve this fundamental argument. In the literature about emotional intelligence there is a strong consensus that it is a developable trait or competency and a lot of the popular literature is devoted to describing processes or programmes which are designed to help individuals develop their emotional intelligence. However, some issues do arise about the stage in an individual's life at which interventions designed to build emotional intelligence are most effective. Daniel Goleman comments that, while emotional intelligence is amenable to development, it is interventions during childhood which are most effective and educational research provides the most robust evidence to support such a proposition. Building from this research and extensive case studies, the value of learning emotional intelligence 'skills' during childhood is promoted. However some doubts have been raised about the effectiveness of development action at later stages in life.

The significance of the potential value of emotional intelligence within an organisational context has led to a range of discussions about its role and development within a managerial learning context. Indeed many authors point out that although the core emotional intelligence capabilities are developed within childhood, these are plastic and are capable of being developed and changed. Workplace experiences also have a significant impact on this shaping process – what managers learn in an organisation includes 'how to feel about what they do and learn'. The emotional dimension of the work of management is reflected through working experiences and practices.

Developing or Exploiting?

As just noted, within the overall debate on the nature of emotional intelligence, there has been considerable discussion around the issue of the extent to which EI can be developed. In broad terms there is an emerging consensus that EI can be developed, but there are differing views on the extent of development possible. We had initially thought that some elements could be more readily developed than others and proposed that 'Enablers' are more amenable to development than 'Constrainers' or 'Drivers' but our views have changed in the light of our research evidence.

When thinking about development, we like to use the analogy of a person's capacity as a vessel containing fluid to illustrate the development of elements of EI. The overall capacity of some elements we believe can be increased through training by extending the range of an individual's skills.

This is what we refer to as being 'Developable'. At the other extreme, some elements appear to be more enduring characteristics, probably formed earlier in life, and so could be seen as vessels that are fixed in size. Therefore, experience can only increase the volume of contents within the vessel, not the size of the vessel itself. This is what we mean by 'Exploiting' one's capacity. On the basis of our own research, we now believe that the seven elements lie on a development continuum ranging from: 'Easily Developable, Malleable' through to 'Difficult to Develop', need to exploit one's capacity formed earlier in life.

We have found in some studies that unusual work or other experiences have encouraged some individuals to exploit their existing capacities for Conscientiousness and Intuitiveness. In another study, in which managers received EI training, the results of re-testing showed that some Enablers – Self-awareness, Influence and Sensitivity – had improved after training, as we had predicted, but so too had Motivation and Resilience. Using the vessel analogy presented above, an individual's overall capacity for Motivation and Resilience could be seen to have increased through training.

Our initial view that the scores of the Drivers and Enablers are unlikely to change over time has been supported, at least in part, by our findings. Intuitiveness and Conscientiousness did not improve after training, and so can be seen as vessels which are fixed in size – experience can only increase the volume of contents within the vessel. However, results from other studies show that Intuitiveness and Conscientiousness can be improved through experience, i.e. team leaders, and skippers and successful crews in the Global Challenge Yacht Race. This is what 'Exploiting' one's capacity means. The other two elements, Emotional Resilience and Intuitiveness, which we had previously considered to be only 'Exploitable' had also shown improvements after training and so probably lie between these two extremes. An overview of development action incorporating a continuum of 'Develop – Exploit' is shown in **Table 7.1**, but further research is needed to confirm these propositions. Nevertheless, there is certainly support for the proposition that EI can, to a certain extent, be developed. This has implications for organisations in terms of the nature and design of development activities, which we deal with in the next section. Given the evidence that EI is related to performance, it would seem reasonable to assume that organisations would be interested in devising programmes and processes designed to develop the levels of EI of their people.

Table 7.1: EI Elements: The 'Develop – Exploit' Continuum

EIQ Elements	Develop	←--------------→	Exploit
Personal Enablers Self-awareness Emotional Resilience Intuitiveness	✔	✔	✔
Inter-Personal Enablers Inter-personal Sensitivity Influence	✔ ✔		
Driver Motivation		✔	
Constrainer Conscientiousness			✔

An Overall Development Framework

With any personal development activity it is essential to adopt a planned approach in order to be able to sustain the activity. **Figure 7.1** provides a framework for a planned approach to developing emotional intelligence.

Figure 7.1: Development Framework

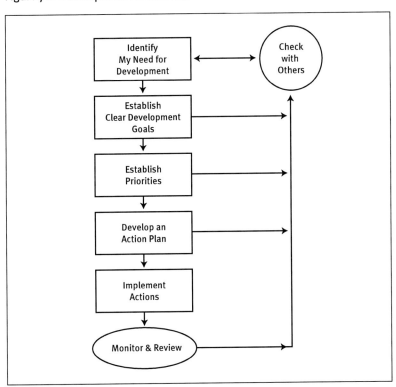

The key steps in this approach are discussed below.

Step 1: Identify My Need for Development

If you completed the brief self-assessment in **chapter 6,** you have already made a start. Reflecting on your own strengths and weaknesses is a critical first step in the development process. As an initial exercise, spend some time filling out an emotional intelligence inventory. A potential format for this is shown in **Table 7.2.**

Table 7.2: Emotional Intelligence Inventory

Emotional Intelligence Element	My Strengths are	Examples	My Weaknesses are	Examples
Self-awareness				
Emotional Resilience				
Motivation				
Interpersonal Sensitivity				
Influence				
Intuitiveness				
Conscientiousness				

To complete this inventory you should look back over the descriptions of the seven elements of emotional intelligence in **chapters 3** and **5** and your earlier self-assessment. No doubt, unless you are a truly exceptional person, you will be able to identify some strengths and weaknesses in relation to each of the elements. In doing this, note down specific examples of actions and behaviours which you believe demonstrate your strengths and weaknesses. To get the most from this exercise it is very important to be as honest with yourself as possible. The more specific you can be in describing examples the more helpful you will find them when it comes to later steps in the overall development process.

This is a valuable (even vital) first step, but it only represents your own view. If you have completed an assessment of emotional intelligence (e.g. the EIQ: M) you can use the results as further evidence of your strengths and weaknesses. You may also have completed other personality questionnaires during your career (for example the Myers Briggs Type Inventory, the 16PF, or the OPQ). If you have, then reviewing this information will help you in building a more accurate initial inventory. At this stage we are focusing on developing emotional intelligence in a work context. A further source of help would be notes from past job performance or career review discussions.

To a large extent emotional intelligence is exhibited in your interactions with other people, so you should obtain input from other people. Spend time with others you work with (for example colleagues, your boss, customers, etc.) reviewing your initial draft inventory and obtaining their reactions and perceptions. This not only helps you to obtain a more accurate initial inventory, but can also be a valuable development activity in its own right. If you do not feel comfortable having such discussions with work colleagues it is important to get some form of 'independent' perspective from another person – someone who knows you well and who you can trust from outside work (a friend, relative, partner, etc.).

The need for a third party perspective is important throughout the development process. To help to achieve this, explain the whole process to those you are talking to and try to get one or two of them to agree to act as 'guides' at later stages. Given the nature of the overall development framework at least one of these 'guides' should know you in a work context.

Step 2: Establish Clear Development Goals

Having formulated a profile of your strengths and weaknesses in terms of emotional intelligence the next important step is to determine how you would like to improve. At this stage it is worth exploring each of the elements separately. The question you should have in mind during this exploration is:

What types of behaviour would I like to be displaying in relation to this element of emotional intelligence?

Answering this question requires more than saying 'I would like to overcome all of the weaknesses'. You must develop a clear, and inspiring picture of how you would really like to be in terms of actions and behaviours associated with each element. It is really helpful to be aspirational at this step. Think of what you would really like to be in terms of the elements rather than the level of improvement you feel you can comfortably achieve. **Figure 7.2** illustrates diagrammatically how we can achieve more growth by thinking aspirationally and adjusting to reality rather than thinking incrementally.

Figure 7.2: Aspirational vs Incremental

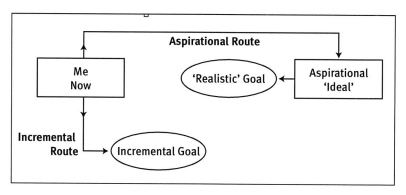

You should identify some 'role models' when developing the 'aspirational' picture for each of the elements. Identifying individuals who represent a really desirable set of behaviours in relation to each of the elements of emotional intelligence helps to make more concrete the changes in behaviour which you could give yourself as a target. It is unlikely that any single individual will represent a 'role model' for all seven of the elements of emotional intelligence so you need to consider who, for you, represents a 'role model' for each element. This process of focusing on an individual is more valuable if it is someone you know, or have contact with, at work. What you are looking for at this stage is to be able to describe, in concrete terms, the actions and behaviours which you would like to be able to replicate. Although we have been focusing our discussion of emotional intelligence in a work context it is possible (and perhaps desirable) to look for role models in a non-work situation. This way, we can examine the behaviours in both work and non-work contexts.

Once again the discipline of writing down your thoughts and ideas in a structured way is a valuable aid to development planning. A possible framework for this is shown in **Table 7.3**. Discussing your developmental goals with the 'guide(s)' you agreed to work with during Step 1 can help to ensure that you have been realistic and clear in describing the change you would like to achieve in the development process. The discussions with the 'guide(s)' are much more valuable if you are both familiar with the selected 'role models'. Failing that, you should provide your 'guide' with a vivid description of your 'role model's' behaviours and the reasons why you selected them to illustrate the element of emotional intelligence you are considering.

Table 7.3: Development Goals

Emotional Intelligence Element	'Role Model'	Behaviours the 'Role Model' Exhibits	Behaviours which Comprise my Development Goal
Self-awareness			
Emotional Resilience			
Motivation			
Interpersonal Sensitivity			
Influence			
Intuitiveness			
Conscientiousness			

When you have completed this step in the process, you should have a clear picture of 'where you are' and 'where you want to be' in terms of developing your emotional intelligence.

Step 3: Establishing Priorities

On completion of Step 2, many of us are likely to be faced with a challenging agenda for personal development and change. There can be little doubt that setting out to develop our emotional intelligence represents a significant change initiative. To achieve success it is important that:

- you have a clear and compelling reason to change (this could either be a desire or a requirement)

- you have a clear picture of the desired end point

- you can see and understand actions which will lead you to the desired end point

- you have early experience of success which you can see moving you towards the end point.

The earlier chapters in this book, together with Steps 1 and 2 above, should have addressed the first two criteria. The overall development process is designed to address the third criterion (and we will return to this later). However, at the end of Step 2 we are facing a significant range of potential development needs and goals. To meet the fourth, it is important to establish some development priorities. If we fail to do this then we run the risk of being 'swamped' by the magnitude of the task (unless we have outstanding emotional resilience) and will not implement our personal development and change process. One way of avoiding this is to establish an action priority list which is likely to produce early results and which in turn will motivate us to sustain our efforts.

There are many ways in which a range of actions may be prioritised. However, in the context of change, prioritising in a way which produces early results is important to reinforce the commitment to change and thus sustain the effort. **Figure 7.3** illustrates a framework for prioritising actions in a change context which is particularly helpful in planning to develop emotional intelligence.

Figure 7.3: Prioritising Change

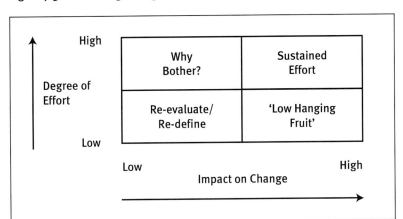

Having developed a picture of the development goals, each should be assessed and positioned on the matrix. Those which come out as a Low:Low should be re-analysed. These areas may not be related to the development of your emotional intelligence or have been undervalued in terms of their difficulty or impact. Those which require considerable effort, but are likely to have little impact are potential distractors. They could be re-visited once everything else has been done, but should not be allowed to detract from effort which you should be devoting to those areas which will have a notable impact on the development of your emotional intelligence. The goals which require little effort, but are likely to have a high impact, tend to represent those areas of action where you are tempted to say 'Why on earth haven't I done something about this before?'. Focus on these at an early stage. The results will provide you with the reinforcement and motivation required for the sustained effort to address those goals which fall into the high effort, high impact quadrant.

Once again discussing and testing your own analysis with your 'guide(s)' can be of great value in ensuring that you arrive at a realistic assessment of development priorities.

Step 4: Developing an Action Plan

Once you have a clear view of your development needs and priorities it is necessary to identify the actions which you can take to underpin and realise these goals. This takes us back to the earlier questions about the relationship between the elements of emotional intelligence and their developability or necessity to exploit personal characteristics. Later sections in this chapter present development prompts and ideas which may be appropriate for each of the elements of emotional intelligence. However, it is worth, reflecting on the general considerations which can apply to developmental and exploiting strategies. Common to both aspects is the importance of **feedback**. Whether planning to develop new behaviours or exploit (and develop strategies for coping with core aspects of your personality) it is important to begin the process by considering how you manage behavioural feedback. There are two elements to this aspect of development planning which are:

- Learning how to use and interpret feedback from others; and

- Actively seeking feedback

In formulating an action plan it is important to build in processes and frameworks for seeking and interpreting feedback.

You must encourage regular and open feedback from others on how your behaviours are being perceived and interpreted as it is only through the perceptions of others that you are able to evaluate the effectiveness of your actions in terms of achieving your goals. Thus any action plan you formulate should include an element which shows how you will seek and gather feedback from others. Receiving feedback is important. How you evaluate and respond to this feedback can be critical. In evaluating feedback it is critical to have an open mind. You need to look for patterns in the feedback you receive in relation to your self-perceptions. In broad terms, it is necessary to look for patterns in feedback which is derived from different sources. The greater the degree of congruence of the feedback, the more likely it is to be providing a 'true' picture of how others perceive you. Any development plans should include processes to gather, review, evaluate and respond to feedback from others.

In broad terms, if development needs relate to 'developable' components of emotional intelligence then your action plan should focus on learning activities. For many of the elements which fall into these categories there are a range of interventions which are well established and readily available (for example training programmes focusing on negotiation skills or influencing skills). Those areas requiring 'coping' strategies which relate to the individual's personal characteristics are more difficult to plan for. While many of these areas can be addressed in the longer-term through psychoanalytic approaches there is little available which provides short-term results. In reality, people develop effective strategies for coping with personal shortcomings and playing to their strengths to counteract these. For example, intuitiveness (as an element of emotional intelligence) is in the area of a personal characteristic. If an individual is low on this element a potential coping strategy may be to work on key decisions in a group or team context and to ensure that processes entail thorough risk assessment techniques with the formulation of clear up-front decision criteria. The combination of these two actions lead to a higher degree of comfort in arriving at a clear decision. From the above illustration it is clear that the 'exploitable' strategies require:

- Identification of personal areas of discomfort
- Development of processes to examine and cover each area of discomfort
- Achievement of a decision or action in a context different to that of discomfort

The range of specific actions for each development goal need to be considered in terms of:

- What has to be achieved?

- What do I need to do?

- What resources/support do I need to enable me to do this?

- How long will it take to achieve meaningful results?

Developing an effective action plan is helped by formalising it and discussing it with others. A possible format for an action plan is shown in **Table 7.4**. Once again, considerable value can be obtained from discussing and reviewing the action plan with your 'guide(s)'. In a work context, it is important to review and discuss the action plan with those who need to support you or provide resources (particularly your immediate boss).

Table 7.4: Action Plan

Element of Emotional Intelligence	Development Goal	Development Actions	Support/ Resources	Timescale
Self-awareness				
Emotional Resilience				
Motivation				
Interpersonal Sensitivity				
Influence				
Intuitiveness				
Conscientiousness				

Stage 5: Implement Actions

This stage requires that you implement those actions to which you committed. This is the stage that requires personal commitment. The relationship you have established with your 'guide(s)' can be helpful at this stage. In developing the 'guide' relationship, it can be particularly helpful to empower the 'guide(s)' to challenge and question you or your progress in implementing your agreed actions.

Stage 6: Monitor and Review

It is very important to continue the process of self-analysis and the regular gathering and review of feedback on your actions and behaviours in order to evaluate the effectiveness of your development actions. You should actively seek feedback from all your sources to track how your development initiatives have led to real changes in your behaviours.

The feedback from this review should be used not only to check on the effectiveness of your development actions, but also to help you to formulate a further development plan.

Development Ideas

General Development Ideas

The nature of emotional intelligence is such that it is possible to enhance the overall level by planned and sustained personal development. Much of this development will result from the individual reflecting on the behaviours you tend to exhibit in differing situations, consciously practising different behaviours and actively seeking feedback on the way in which others interpret and respond to these new behaviours.

In broad terms it is important to reflect on how the feedback might apply in a range of situations which you have faced and to recapture and reflect on these. When reviewing your feedback, and to identify development ideas, it is useful to think about a recent situation or decision and to consider the following questions:

- What were your feelings in this situation?

- How did you feel about the outcomes of your actions?

- How could the outcomes have been improved in terms of the solution of the problem/situation?

- How could the outcomes have been improved in terms of your feelings?

- What have you learned from this situation which could help you in dealing with future issues?

Within this overall approach it is important that you examine each of the emotional intelligence scales and identify those where:

(a) you have strengths which may be developed and generalised;

(b) there are specific opportunities for improvement.

The following sections provide some general questions and thoughts to help you develop behaviours which will enhance your performance in relation to each of the elements of emotional intelligence.

Ideas for Developing and Exploiting the Seven Elements

A Self-awareness

In examining the self-awareness scale it is important to be reflective in terms of behaviour. You may be helped by the following prompts.

- Reflect on specific situations/problems which you have faced

  - how did you feel?

  - what concerned you?

  - what excited you?

  - how did the reactions of others affect your feelings?

- How did you decide your actions?

- How consciously did you take account of your feelings and emotions?

- How would your responses and actions have been different if you had been aware of them?

- Based on this reflection, how can you improve your reactions and solutions in the future?

B *Emotional Resilience*

Thoughts and ideas which can be helpful in exploiting emotional resilience include:

- Reflect on how you adapt your behaviours to deal with different situations

- Develop an understanding of how decisions are made and the balance between objective certainty and the need to arrive at judgements based on a balance of probabilities

- Identify situations presenting difficult decision-options and reflect on behaviours you adopted in such situations which led to successful outcomes

- When faced with challenge spend time openly exploring the reason for it and seek opportunities to learn from such discussions

- Actively seek opportunities to involve others in exploring solutions to difficult problems or situations.

C *Motivation*

It is difficult to approach motivation in the same way as other areas of behaviour. It is important that you understand your own motivation and develop strategies to **exploit** this. The following prompts may be helpful.

- Develop a clear understanding of results and goals relating to the work situations and problems you find

- Analyse potential for personal satisfaction and benefits which would flow from effective solution of problems

- Reflect on situations in which you have felt a high degree of personal motivation and identify elements which may be transferred to other situations and/or generalised as work behaviours

- Identify/build a clear picture of your personal goals/aims and establish ways in which work situations may support their achievement. Discuss your analysis with a mentor or 'uninvolved' third party.

D *Interpersonal Sensitivity*

While there are a range of interventions which can be effective in building interpersonal sensitivity, it is important for you to identify actions which can be readily undertaken in a work context. Ideas to explore include:

- Spend time discussing problems and situations with team members, invite their comments and spend time reflecting on how their comments throw light on the problem

- Make active use of a mentor to discuss work problems or situations and your interpretations of them, and of your preferred solutions on those you work with. In developing a plan or course of action, spend time reflecting on how your ideas may be perceived by those involved with or *supported* by the action

- Reflect on situations in which you feel that you have really achieved *'buy-in'* for others and identify ways in which you can generalise the behaviours you exhibited

- Spend time listening to others; begin by posing a problem or outlining a situation and asking for their input *before* presenting your view

- Use questions or interaction with others rather than making statements

- How much time do you spend on getting to know your co-workers and how actively do you attempt to bring their reactions to bear in understanding your own motives and actions?

E Influence

As with interpersonal sensitivity there are a range of established development interventions or courses which can assist in building influencing skills. However, it can be helpful to use the following prompts to help you think about actions to develop your behaviours in this area.

- Spend time understanding the perspectives of others

- Examine issues, problems and situations, and hypothesise what they might be like from the perspective of Mr X, Ms Y, etc.

- What do others need from their job, relationships with me, etc.?

- Reflect on how well I understand those I am working with.

F Intuitiveness

Developing intuitiveness raises similar issues to those mentioned in connection with motivation. Some ideas to raise which can help you to develop strategies to exploit your intuitiveness are:

- Develop an understanding of how you can assess and manage risks in decision making

- Reflect on decisions which you have made in difficult situations and consider how alternative decisions may have 'played out' in practice

- Spend time discussing complex decisions with others involved with, or impacted by, them

- Consider how further information would have impacted on past decisions

- When faced with difficult decisions reflect on options and potential improvements resulting from further analysis before undertaking the analysis

- Develop an understanding of the processes of arriving at business decisions.

G *Conscientiousness*

This element reflects a core trait and needs (like motivation and intuitiveness) you to exploit your level of conscientiousness. Ideas and prompts to use in reflecting on this element include:

- Obtain feedback from others to establish the requisite level of consistency between what you say and what you do

- Only openly commit to goals and decisions that you feel are important and can be delivered

- Identify how others judge your commitment to decisions and actions

- Establish a clear and rigorous approach to establishing priorities and ensure that you apply this in practice

- Ensure that you create time to deliver your contribution to high priority actions.

The above suggestions have a strong focus on what should be examined in relation to the development of each of the seven elements of emotional intelligence, but only touch on the question of 'how' very briefly. However, the development of emotional intelligence is, in our view, best approached as a part of a process of personal development. In this context we feel that the keys to development relate to the willingness to undertake a sustained development process rather than seeking a 'quick fix'. This in turn requires that the individual undertaking the development is willing and motivated to change and to take ownership of the development process and its direction. The framework described earlier in the chapter, we believe, helps the individual to do this. However, if you want to undertake the development of your emotional intelligence you can benefit (and indeed probably need support) from others. The areas in which you are likely to need support are:

- *Obtaining feedback* Try to ensure that you can work with an individual, whose opinions and views you trust, and explain your goals to them. Then ask them to provide you with honest and open feedback on the extent to which you are exhibiting the behaviours you seek to develop.

- *Keeping on track* Most of us have experienced the initial enthusiasm of starting on the process of implementing a New Year's resolution. Equally most of us have relapsed. A common resolution is to lose weight, yet research suggests that fewer than 5 per cent of individuals who undertake a diet maintain their weight loss. This statistic changes significantly when individuals are confronted with the consequences of relapses in their plan (hence the success of organisations such as Weight-Watchers and, even more significantly, Alcoholics Anonymous). The lesson from this is to set in place mechanisms to prevent relapse. Again the use of a trusted mentor or guide can help you with this.

- *Practice* In any behaviour change process it is essential to practise new behaviours. In developing emotional intelligence it is important to find a range of situations in which you can practice the targeted behaviours you want to change. Try to ensure that you select situations from which you can obtain feedback, since practice without feedback does little to help in building new behaviours.

- *Monitor and evaluate change* Look for ways of evaluating the extent to which you have been successful in making the changes you set out to achieve. This can be by means of informal feedback or (after say six to twelve months) re-taking an emotional intelligence assessment to monitor the extent to which your rating on the elements you set out to change have been successful.

Is There a Course?

In working with individuals and organisations on the assessment of emotional intelligence and its development we have often been confronted with questions such as:

We hear what you say about no 'quick fixes', but there must be a course we can attend to help us. Which one is it?

We genuinely cannot answer this question. The sheer popularity and high profile of the topic has spawned a myriad of courses and seminars claiming either to build emotional intelligence or at least to contribute to its development. It is beyond the scope of this book (and our legal expenses insurance!) to comment on specific courses and their claims. However, it is worth emphasising that a number of the elements of emotional intelligence are amenable to specific skill development which may be helped by a training course (e.g. influencing skills). However, other elements which can be developed may be assisted by broader-based training programmes. For example, the relatively recent growth in training Neuro Linguistic Programming (NLP) appears to be relevant to the development of emotional intelligence. Exploring NLP training as a specific tool it is worth reflecting on a definition of NLP provided by Joseph O'Connor and John Seymour.

'... the art and science of excellence, derived from studying how top people in different fields obtain their outstanding results.'

The resonance between this definition and the view of the significance of emotional intelligence as a determinant of success indicates that NLP training could be very helpful in building emotional intelligence. Indeed further investigation into what NLP explores and develops shows the importance of:

- Motivation
- Self-awareness

- Interpersonal Sensitivity
- Emotional Resilience and
- Influence

These linkages are summarised in **Table 7.5.**

Table 7.5: NLP Concepts and Emotional Intelligence Elements

NLP Concept	Emotional Intelligence Element
Outcomes	Motivation, Emotional Resilience
Rapport	Interpersonal Sensitivity, Influence
Communication Skills	Influence
Pacing and Levelry	Influence, Interpersonal Sensitivity
Doors of Perception	Self-awareness

Although NLP training is clearly a valuable tool in developing emotional intelligence it does not represent a 'quick fix'. Building NLP skills requires sustained effort to achieve personal development goals and thus may be seen as aligned to emotional intelligence in its developmental philosophy.

A training 'approach' or 'model' somewhat older than NLP is that of Transactional Analysis (TA). TA is built on a Freudian model of communication. At its heart, the TA model examines the breakdown of communications resulting from 'crossed transactions'. This means that one individual is engaging in a transaction in one 'mental state' while the other responds from another. The initial work on TA was carried out in the world of group therapy by exponents such as Eric Berne and Thomas Harris. They identified that in interacting with others we use one of three 'mental states'. These they labelled as Parent, Adult and Child. The three states correspond directly to Freud's Id, Ego and Super-Ego; with Id being the Child, Ego the Adult and Super-Ego the Parent. In broad terms TA training is designed to help individuals develop effective transactions by minimising (through self-awareness and awareness of others) 'crossed transactions' and raising interactions to the complimentary Adult to Adult level. TA training addresses the emotional intelligence elements of interpersonal sensitivity, self-awareness and influence. However, as with NLP, TA training requires a sustained approach to personal development rather than a 'quick fix'.

From the brief descriptions of two major established training frameworks it is evident that, while they can address a significant component of the development of emotional intelligence, they also share a common view that change will result from personal development which requires sustained effort.

This chapter has hopefully provided the reader with reassurance that much of emotional intelligence is capable of development. Equally it should have provided the reassurance (or possible concern!) that there is no instant transformation available through a 'quick fix' course which people aren't telling you about. If you really are motivated to develop your emotional intelligence you can do it but you need to recognise that such a development is part of your overall development. The first step on the journey to build your emotional intelligence is a genuine recognition of the need combined with the genuine desire to improve. Once you have made the first step you will be able to manage the subsequent ones.

Emotional Intelligence and Leadership

Introduction

We have already highlighted the enormous growth in interest in the idea of emotional intelligence over the last few years (**chapter 1**). Over the last decade there has been an explosive growth in the level of interest in leadership within organisations. One leading researcher pointed out that in the 1980s around 1,000 articles and papers were published each year in the area of leadership but by the late 1990s this figure had risen to somewhere in the region of 8,000! It was estimated that in 2000/2001, over 3,500 books on the topic were published. Leadership is clearly a 'hot topic'. What is evident from the previous chapters is that **not all leaders have high emotional intelligence**. However, not all leaders are really successful in the long-term. In many organisational contexts there is a need for successful leaders to possess high emotional intelligence. Given what we read about the changing nature of the business environment, this need will increase. In spite of the growing level of interest in leadership we seem to be no closer to understanding what leadership is really about.

Leadership seems to be a 'black box' or a mysterious concept. Every time an attempt is made to define what makes for effective leadership the results present us with contradictions and draw many to the conclusion that great leaders are 'born and not made'. One leading writer in this field (Manfred Kets de Vries) has, rather aptly, commented that:

'When we plunge into the organisational literature on leadership, we quickly become lost in a labyrinth: there are endless definitions, countless articles and never-ending polemics. As far as leadership studies go, it seems that more and more has been studied about less and less, to end up ironically with a group of researchers who studied everything about nothing. It prompted one wit to say recently that reading the current world literature on leadership is rather like going through the Parisian telephone directory while trying to read it in Chinese!'

Why is there a Growing Interest in Leadership?

Given the difficulty in pinning down the concept it is worth asking the question 'why the interest?' What is clear is that there are real business drivers, which seem to be:

- *The Talent Wars.* Evidence is emerging that organisations perceive the key to sustainable competitive advantage as being intricately involved with the ability to attract and retain a critical mass of talent in a world in which there is a shortage of the required talent.

- *A notable shift in the factors which drive investor decisions.* During the 1960s to the early 1990s, investor behaviour was dominated by 'hard' earnings data. However, since 1990 other 'intangible' factors have influenced this behaviour. In terms of these intangibles, investor views on the leadership of the organisation play a significant role.

- *To compete in a rapidly changing environment, the ability to lead and manage change is a critical success factor.* Yet authors such as John Kotter have estimated that some 70 per cent of change initiatives fail.

The Historic Background

Although the level of interest in the idea of leadership and understanding what makes for effective leadership is at an all time high researchers, writers and observers have, for a long time, noted that top level leaders do make a difference. The academic research in this field has evolved based on the failures of previous frameworks to provide a clear explanation of what it takes to be a great leader. In the 1930s and 1940s the focus was on examining the traits and characteristics associated with 'Great Men'. Interestingly, in this context leadership was perceived as a predominantly male characteristic or attribute. This approach to trying to understand leadership was based on attempting to tie down the common personality traits or characteristics associated with a range of figures (in both commerce and politics) who were widely perceived as 'great leaders'. However, the results of this approach were somewhat confusing and often contradictory. No clear or consistent pattern emerged and the conclusion was drawn that leadership could not be understood or predicted and leaders emerged, rather than resulted, from a clear pattern of behaviours or development. The failure of this 'Great Man' approach to offer help to organisations coincided with a general focus on behaviourist thinking within organisations. This led to a second phase of leadership thinking and research which may be broadly labelled as being a 'behavioural/style' approach. In essence, this was based on the premise that leadership was related to the behaviour and interpersonal style of leaders. The research and writing in this period (dominant in the 1960s) focused on linking humanistic models of work and organisational behaviour to leadership. Once again the results of the research and reported studies were somewhat inconclusive and contradictory.

The continuing interest in attempting to understand the behaviours or characteristics associated with effective leadership led to a focus on exploring the context within which leadership is exercised. During the 1970s this change of focus led to leadership being seen as being situationally or contextually determined. Within this framework the nature of effective leadership was seen as being related to the leader's ability to adapt their behaviours to the needs of specific individuals or the context within which they were operating. However, all of these views of the nature of leadership were focusing purely on the interaction between individuals rather than considering the requirements of the business or organisation. Thus leadership was, in essence, being seen as a higher order set of *enduring* personal skills or characteristics rather than as a means of achieving important longer-term organisational goals. During this somewhat lengthy period, the focus of attention was on the characteristics of the individual who was the designated leader. This tended, largely, to ignore the needs, interests and behaviours of these who 'were being led'. The interaction between leaders and their followers was substantially examined as a one-way process rather than an interactive or iterative one. During the last decade, the association of leadership with organisational success became prevalent due to the links between the outstanding performance, at the time, of a number of companies with a high profile Chief Executive (e.g. Bill Gates at Microsoft, Richard Branson at Virgin, Anita Roddick at Body Shop, Jack Welsh at General Electric).

What is also clear, from the information available is that different organisations in differing business contexts, need different types of leaders. However, when we look at the elements which comprise emotional intelligence, we see that different elements assume differing significance in changing situations while leaders face differing contexts in which they operate.

This obsession with top leadership qualities has led to a refocusing of leadership research on 'top leaders'. The public profile of organisational leaders has always been higher in the US than in the rest of the world. As a result, more recent leadership research has been both focused on US corporations and the top leadership teams. This focus has produced even more emphasis on personal qualities and on charismatic aspects of leadership. However, such bias is not without merit as it has provided some valuable insights into the behavioural aspects of outstanding leadership (in terms of producing significant organisational performance or transformation).

However, an exclusive focus on the top leaders can also be misleading. Many of the 'star' CEOs in the US have subsequently been seen as flawed characters. For example both Kenneth Ley of Enron and Bernie Webbers of Worldcom moved rapidly from role models to 'rogues' in 2002 amid allegations of fraud and business irregularities.

Leadership or Management?

The historic inability to 'pin down' what is meant by leadership has led to a focus on developing effective management within organisations. During the 1960s, 1970s and early 1980s, organisations focused on building managerial competence as a means of securing competitive advantage. This resulted from the inability to *explain*, *predict* and thus be able to develop leadership. The managerial paradigm was much more suited to a rational approach to explanation, analysis and subsequent development than the more subjective and emotional concept of leadership. In the late 1990s, the resurging interest in leadership led to a perceived need to define the differences between leadership and management. While there are numerous and elaborate attempts to establish the differences, Peter Senge captured the essence of the difference in the statement that:

> *'Managers do things right.*
> *Leaders do the right things.'*

This simple, but powerful, statement suggests that managers are focused on conformity, compliance, direction and control. On the other hand leaders are focused on possibilities, uncertainties, opportunities, vision and facilitating the contribution of others to build a successful business. In thinking about leadership and emotional intelligence it may be helpful to review the differences between leadership and management summarised in **Table 8.1**.

Table 8.1: Differences between Leadership and Management

Leadership	Management
• Developing the vision of the future business • Describing the path to achieve the vision • Communicating the vision and path to all employees • Motivating employees to achieve the long-term goals • Managing organisational change and transformation	• Implementation and application • Efficient and effective deployment of resources within business units • Controlling • Monitoring and reviewing performance

Such a distinction invites the viewpoint that leadership is dynamic, positive and good, while management is negative, constraining and bureaucratic. In exploring the need for and nature of leadership in organisations the focus has been on seeking an alternative to the somewhat negative managerial paradigm. This viewpoint is exaggerated when the media present leadership in the context of exciting and attractive entrepreneurial figures such as Richard Branson of Virgin.

However, in reality, it is evident that a truly successful organisation requires a combination of inspirational leadership with managerial effectiveness. If leaders are the organisation visionaries, then their relationship to managers may best be summed up by the established saying that: 'Vision without action is a dream. Action without vision is a nightmare.'

At the beginning of the 21st century we should recognise that a successful organisation needs both leadership and management. However, it may be that both dimensions need to be incorporated within individuals in influential or leading positions. Thus leadership needs to be seen more as a set of behaviours and overall style of working than position within the organisation.

Perhaps effective leadership needs to be viewed as combining vision and action. The concept of the leader/manager is perhaps what we need to be looking at as we move further into the new millennium.

Leadership and Change

There is a growing realisation that the major issue facing organisations is that of managing continuing change. Increasingly, organisations are facing the reality that the future is not one of incremental improvement or adjustment, but rather one of radical change or re-invention of the business. In the UK a decade ago it would have been difficult to have envisaged public sector utilities dealing in the monopolistic provision of a single utility service such as gas or electricity having to position themselves as being a competitive provider of multi-utilities operating on a global scale. Such is the degree of change facing organisations today. However, the evidence of organisations' ability to cope effectively with radical change is somewhat limited. To lead an organisation through such a change process takes considerable skill, ability and personal commitment.

The research into successful leadership of significant change suggests that there are a number of important requirements. A leading researcher and writer in this field, John Kotter, has suggested that the main steps involved are:

1. *Establishing a sense of urgency.* In essence, making the case for change and the need to act quickly.
2. *Forming a powerful coalition.* Ensuring that key players are working together to lead the change effort.
3. *Creating a vision.* Ensuring that a clear picture of the desired and possible future is established and an overall means of realising this vision is established.
4. *Communicating the vision.* Working actively to ensure that everyone in the organisation understands the new vision and the strategies for achieving it.

5. *Empowering others to act on the vision.* Having established and communicated the vision, working to enable others to contribute to its realisation and removing barriers to change. This entails encouraging new ways of behaving and rewarding those who respond to the challenge.

6. *Planning for creating short-term wins.* Ensuring that the results of actions in line with the vision are clearly visible and are planned to result in performance improvements. In addition ensuring that such actions and their results are publicised and visibly acknowledged.

7. *Consolidating improvements and producing still more change.* Building on the 'early wins' and their value to encourage greater effort to pursue the change goals. Publicly acknowledging and promoting those who are contributing to the new vision and to securing significant changes.

8. *Institutionalising new approaches.* Ensuring that all are aware of the relationship between new behaviours and the success of the organisation. Actively working to develop and promote those with the skills and abilities to engage others in the change process.

These components in successful organisational transformation imply a leadership requirement which goes beyond 'traditional' thinking. It is evident that while those seen as leaders, in a conventional sense, must play a major role in the transformation, there is a need for a more dispersed level of 'leadership capability' in an organisation undergoing significant change.

In practice, one of the main focuses of the current interest in leadership relates to the link between leadership and the ability of an organisation to manage and deliver significant organisational change. However, in spite of identifying generic delivery failures, authors tend to avoid specifics in terms of alternative leadership behaviour patterns. Perhaps the issue in addressing proposed routes forward lies with a belief in the role of individual leaders, as an enduring and pervasive set of behaviours, rather than linking leadership behaviours to specific activities in the work involved in making change happen. In a study of change leaders in a large multi-national company, Malcolm Higgs and Deborah Rowland identified a distinct set of leadership competencies that were associated with the work involved in implementing change successfully. These were:

- *Creating the case for change.* Effectively engaging others in recognising the business need for change.

- *Creating structural change.* Ensuring that the change is based on depth of understanding of the issues and supported with a consistent set of tools and processes.

- *Engaging others* in the whole change process and building commitment.

- *Implementing and sustaining changes.* Developing effective plans and ensuring good monitoring and review practices are developed.

- *Facilitating and developing capability.* Ensuring that people are challenged to find their own answers and that they are supported in doing this.

Research evidence using this framework has demonstrated the importance of this set of competencies for effective change implementation.

While the research on leadership and change is still an emerging area, there is some evidence that a competence-based framework, combined with planned development, can impact on both business results and the building of leadership capability.

Transformational versus Transactional Leadership

Bass, an influential writer on leadership, outlined a model which distinguished between transactional and transformational leadership. This distinction addresses, to an extent, both the leadership versus manager contribution and the role of leadership in an organisation. In addition, he highlights the relevance of distinction to the change context. In broad terms Bass's model proposed that leadership is

> '... *a transformational influence process, often involving a restructuring of the situation and the perceptions of the members of the organisation.*'

In very broad terms this statement may be understood in terms of:

Transformational leaders do the right things
Transactional leaders do things right.

Transformational leadership is about looking forward and being expansive, while transactional leadership is about the 'here and now' and about focusing on control.

He then proposes that transformational leadership is concerned with:

Charismatic Behaviours: Providing highly esteemed role models whom followers strive to emulate and who align others around a common vision, purpose and sense of direction.

Inspirational Motivation: Motivates and inspires others by providing meaning about the mission and its attainability.

Intellectual Stimulation: Encouraging followers to question basic conceptions and to consider problems from new and unique perspectives. Also encouraging others to be creative and innovative.

Individual Consideration: Paying special attention to each individual's needs for growth and personal achievement. Helping individuals to realise their potential and contribution through coaching and mentoring.

These elements of transformational leadership appear to be concerned with the relationships between the leaders and followers. In addition they seem to be focused on moving people towards the goals that the leader deems to be important. To achieve this movement (based on the construction of effective leader/follower relationships) would appear to call for: influence, intuitiveness, self-awareness, interpersonal sensitivity and motivation – all clearly aspects of emotional intelligence.

This model appears, particularly in relation to the transformational components, to address the leadership requirement for transformational change. However, much of the research into the validity of the model has focused on senior leader behaviours and, like much of the leadership research in the 1990s, has been US dominated.

More recent UK research conducted by Beverly Alimo-Metcalfe (Professor of Leadership at Leeds University) has attempted to capture followers' perceptions of leadership and to explore the leadership behaviour of both those at the top of the organisation (distant leaders) and those exercising dispersed leadership (*nearby* leaders). Based on this substantial UK research she has identified nine transformational leadership factors. These are:

1. *Individualised consideration.* Largely along the lines of the factor proposed by Bass.
2. *Decisive, determined and achieving.* Leaders who make decisions, follow them through and achieve results.

3. *Involves others in discussion and formulation of vision, values and objectives.* Discusses not only the 'what', but also the 'how' and the relationship between the two.

4. *Networks actively, promotes the organisation/team and works closely with a range of stakeholders.*

5. *Empowers individuals and teams to act in line with agreed vision, values and objectives.*

6. *Actively manages changes with sensitivity.* Is aware of the implications for, and impact of the changes, others involved.

7. *Is genuinely accessible to followers.* Makes time available for others and is approachable.

8. *Is intellectually versatile.* Able to operate at a number of different levels ranging from big picture conceptualisation to detailed implementation and action.

9. *Is highly self-aware and acts with integrity.* Is open to input from others and change and able to be honest with himself/herself and others.

Reviewing the above list illustrates some potential links between emotional intelligence and leadership. The list either implies, or directly states, that leadership requires the following elements of emotional intelligence:

- interpersonal sensitivity
- self-awareness
- influence
- conscientiousness
- intuitiveness
- motivation

This expanded version of transformational leadership relates closely to Kotter's views of the requirements for successful change in an organisation. At the same time it proposes a challenging template for successful leadership.

The Leader and the Organisation

In presenting her research on leadership, Beverly Alimo-Metcalfe highlights that the organisational context and situational considerations relating to leadership are not adequately considered. In terms of the leadership setting it is important to balance the organisation's strategy and vision, culture and people with the leadership requirement. This is not purely an analysis of individual components in a state of stasis; rather it is a question of considering how the dynamic equilibrium between these three dimensions is maintained. To a large extent the maintenance of the dynamic equilibrium may be seen as occurring through a process of organisational learning and adjustment. This relationship is summarised in **Figure 8.1**.

Figure 8.1: The Leadership Context

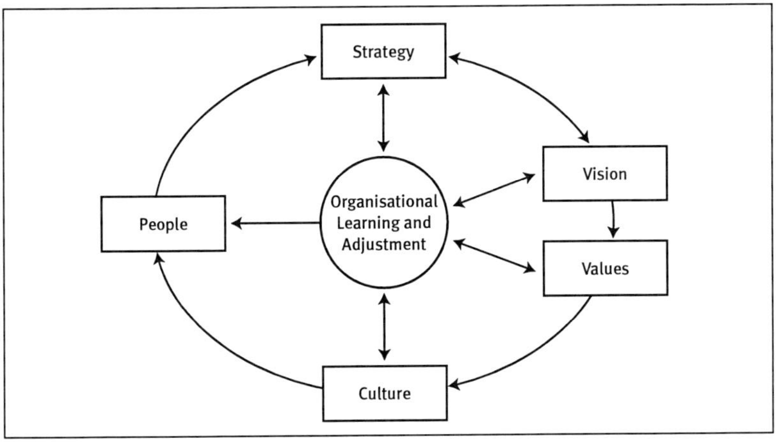

While the leadership context is clearly dynamic the requirement of effective leadership is also **dynamic**. This dynamic requires a balance between the personality or make up of the leader, how the leader behaves, and the overall cognitive models or 'mind maps' the leader works with. An effective leader uses constant feedback from many sources and adapts each component through a process of individual learning. This dynamic is summarised in **Figure 8.2**.

Figure 8.2: The Leadership Requirement

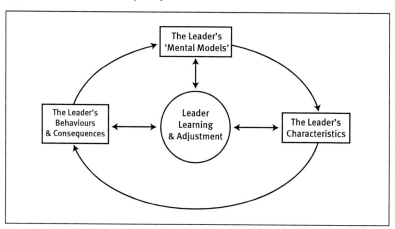

Much of the research and writing on leadership and organisation focuses on one or other of the models outlined in **Figures 8.1** and **8.2**. However, in reality there is a relationship between the two. At the simplest level we can understand that how a leader conceptualises their business world impacts on the formulation of strategy. However, the very conceptualisation of the strategy is eventually impacted by the reality of the organisational learning resulting from its attempted implementation. Thus leaders impact on the organisations and, in a dynamic sense, the reality of the organisational experience impacts on the leaders. This relationship is summarised in **Figure 8.3**.

Leadership is therefore about managing the dynamics between these two viewpoints and ensuring effective performance of both individuals and the organisation.

Within this dynamic model there is an important shift to considering leader behaviours and the ability of leaders to build the capability of their followers to adapt to change and deliver the strategic goals.

Although not explicitly acknowledging this shift in view on the nature of leadership, there is a body of literature which is beginning to look at leadership through a 'new lens' to attempt to make sense of a complex

Figure 8.3: The Dynamics of Leadership

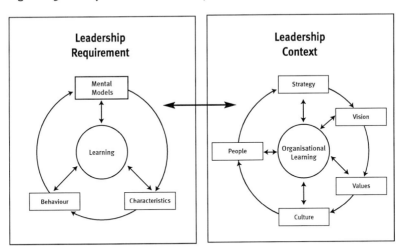

concept in today's business environment. This 'emerging school' encompasses elements of other approaches already described. Within this 'emerging theory' school of thought there are two common strands:

- the focus of study is on what leaders actually do; and

- the determinant of effectiveness includes the leader's impact on followers and their subsequent ability to perform.

It may have been Kotter's study in 1990 which prompted a move from studying personality, or testing theoretical models in the search for understanding of the nature of leadership. His study of the work of leaders is certainly seen to influence many of the studies that may be placed in this 'emerging school'. Typical of these studies is the work reported by Kouzes and Posner, that identified the following elements of effective leadership (with effectiveness judged from the follower's perspective).

- *Challenging the process.* A constant questioning of why things are being done in a certain way combined with openness to having their own actions challenged.

- *Inspiring shared vision.* Engaging others with a vision of how things can be and how progress may be made.

- *Enabling others to act.* Working on a belief in the potential of people and creating the conditions to enable people to realise their potential.

- *Modelling the way.* Acting as a role model and demonstrating integrity in terms of congruence of words and actions.

- *Encouraging the heart.* Providing recognition tailored to an understanding of the needs and personalities of each person.

When reviewing these findings clear overlaps with elements of transformational leadership become apparent. Furthermore, the work of Alimo-Metcalfe applies these transformational concepts in a follower context. However, this does not diminish the potential contribution of Kouzes and Posner when seen in a 'sensemaking' context. A further illustration of the 'emerging school' is provided by the research of Goffee and Jones, who identify the following behaviours of effective leaders:

- *Approachability and vulnerability.* Willingness to expose personal weaknesses thus revealing their humanity approachability.

- *Intuitive in dealing with 'soft' data.* Using 'soft' data to judge the nature and timing of interventions.

- *Tough empathy.* Empathising genuinely, but realistically and caring about what people do.

- *Reveal differences.* Capitalise on what is unique about themselves.

Goffee and Jones are quite explicit in their acknowledgement that a number of 'effective' leaders they studied would not necessarily have been considered so in the absence of the follower's perspective.

When reviewing studies such as those outlined above, it becomes evident that this 'emerging school' sees leadership as being a combination of personal characteristics and areas of competence.

This relatively simple statement has significant implications for the way in which we view leadership. The personality of the leader plays an important part in the exercise of leadership. The areas of effectiveness (the 'skills') need to be exercised in a way that is congruent with the underlying personality of the leader. Building on this view it is possible to suggest a model that reflects the research and thinking on leadership emerging from a 'sensemaking' paradigm. This model is shown in **Figure 8.4**.

Figure 8.4: An Emerging Model of Effective Leadership

• Envision • Engage • Enable • Inquire • Develop	Skills/Competencies
• Authenticity • Integrity • Will • Self-Belief • Self-Awareness	Being Yourself

The elements in this model are explored briefly below:

(a)   Skill/Competence Areas

- *Envision* – the ability to identify a clear future picture which will inform the way in which people direct their efforts and utilise their skills.

- *Engage* – finding the appropriate way for each individual to understand the vision and, hence, the way in which they can contribute.

- *Enable* – acting on a belief in the talent and potential of individuals, and creating the environment in which these can be released.

- *Inquire* – being open to real dialogue with those involved in the organisation and encouraging free and frank debate of all issues.

- *Develop* – working with people to build their capability and help them to make the envisioned contribution.

(b) Personal Characteristics

- *Authenticity* – being genuine and not attempting to 'play a role', not acting in a manipulative way.

- *Integrity* – being consistent in what you say and do.

- *Will* – a drive to lead, and persistence in working towards a goal.

- *Self-belief* – a realistic evaluation of your capabilities and belief that you can achieve required goals.

- *Self-awareness* – a realistic understanding of 'who you are', how you feel and how others see you.

The Linkage with Emotional Intelligence

Over the last few years many have claimed that effective leadership requires high levels of emotional intelligence. For example, Daniel Goleman (a leading proponent of emotional intelligence) claims that while emotional intelligence is more important than IQ and technical skills, the level of importance is even greater for leadership roles. Indeed, in one radio interview he claimed that the higher one progresses in an organisation, the more important emotional intelligence becomes. Such views have been supported by prominent academics in the leadership arena (e.g. Professors Warren Bennis, Roger Gill) and senior businessmen (e.g. Tim Melville-Ross – former Director General of the Institute of Directors – and Sir John Egan – former CEO of Jaguar Cars and BAA).

These claims can be seen as feasible in the light of how we have seen leadership thinking and research developing.

From the above discussion it is evident that, although we cannot produce a concise definition of leadership we can identify a number of important components. Thus, leadership in today's organisation may be seem to be concerned with:

- Focusing on the needs of individuals
- Decisiveness
- Achievement
- Involving and engaging others in formulating vision and values
- Integrating the internal and external stakeholders
- Empowering followers
- Managing change
- Being accessible, available, and open
- Intellectual versatility
- Self-awareness
- Open to feedback and adaptable
- Able to learn
- Having integrity

If these are the requirements of effective leadership then emotional intelligence clearly provides an indication of leadership potential. This relationship is summarised in **Table 8.2**.

Table 8.2: Emotional Intelligence and Leadership

Elements of Emotional Intelligence	Elements of Effective Leadership
• Self-awareness	• Focus on needs of others
• Conscientiousness	• Decisiveness
• Motivation	• Achievement
• Emotional resilience	• Involvement
• Intuitiveness	• Integrating stakeholders
• Influence	• Empower others
• Interpersonal sensitivity	• Manage change
	• Accessible and open
	• Intellectually versatile
	• Self-awareness
	• Open to feedback
	• Able to learn
	• Integrity

In addition to the 'mapping' of the components of emotional intelligence onto the emergent leadership components outlined above, both **Table 8.1** and **Figure 8.1** point to the need for 'balance'. The concept of 'balance' with emotional intelligence has already been explored in **chapter 4**. The view of leadership outlined in this chapter emphasises the importance of achieving this balance. The emerging view of the requirements for effective leadership and the evidence on the nature of emotional intelligence do, to an extent, overlap. **Chapter 5** has provided some insights into the nature of this relationship.

In order to explore the suggestion that emotional intelligence might be related more broadly to leadership, Malcolm Higgs and Deborah Rowland conducted a content analysis of the transformational leadership models and the work of authors classified above as being in the emergent theory area. Based on this work they mapped out emotional intelligence elements on to a range of leadership models. An example of this mapping is shown in **Table 8.3**. From this it is evident that there is a theoretical case for a broader link between emotional intelligence and leadership. To test the relationships empirically they conducted research using the change leaderships competency model (see above) and a measure of emotional intelligence (the EIQ: M) with a sample of 74 managers. The results of this research showed strong relationships between the change leadership competencies and all but one (Intuitiveness) of the elements of emotional intelligence.

Table 8.3; Relationships between Leadership 'Models' and Emotional Intelligence

Elements of emotional intelligence (from Higgs & Dulewicz, 2000)	Leadership Models	
	Bass (1985) Transitional Transformational	Alimo-Metcalfe (1995) Leadership Constructs
Self-awareness		Self-awareness
Emotional Resilience		
Motivation	Charismatic leadership	Achieving, determined
Interpersonal Sensitivity	Individual consideration Charismatic leadership Intellectual stimulation	Consideration for the individual Sensitive change management
Influence	Charismatic leadership Individual consideration	Networking
Intuitiveness	Intellectual stimulation	Decisive, achieving
Conscientiousness	Individual consideration	Integrity and openness

and Frameworks			
Goffee & Jones (2000) Four Factors	**Kouzes & Posner (1998)**	**Kotter (1990) What Leaders Do**	**Bennis (1985)**
Reveal differences Selectively show weaknesses			Develop self-knowledge Develop feedback sources
Tough empathy	Challenges processes Enable others		Balance change and transition Learn from adversity
Tough empathy	Challenge processes Model the way	Motivating and inspiring Setting directions	Role model
Tough empathy Selectively show weaknesses	Challenge processes Inspire shared vision Enable others Model the way Encourage the heart	Aligning people	Open style
Reveal differences Tough empathy	Inspire shared vision Enable others	Aligning people Motivating and inspiring Setting direction	Open style
Intuition	Inspire shared vision Encourage the heart		Capacity to concentrate Curious about innovation
Tough empathy Reveal differences	Model the way Encourage the heart	Aligning people	Role model

Other research that we have conducted has also provided clear initial evidence of a linkage between emotional intelligence and leadership. We found in one study, using a similar method to that we described in **chapter 3**, that CEOs and chairmen had higher levels of both emotional intelligence and IQ than other directors who, in turn, had higher levels of emotional intelligence than senior managers. Another study explored the relationship between emotional intelligence and assessment centre ratings for participants in a senior level public sector centre for identifying top leadership potential. Again this study found important relationships with emotional intelligence as well as IQ and broader specific competencies. While more research is clearly needed we are prompted to speculate that effective leadership may well be a combination of emotional intelligence, IQ and managerial competence. In a similar way to our earlier work we might see the formula for leadership effectiveness (LQ) as being:

$$EQ + IQ + MQ = LQ$$

However, before making too many claims, we need to remember that emotional intelligence is a complex concept which encompasses seven elements. As mentioned earlier, differing situations may require differing balances of these elements to provide effective leadership. For example, in national leadership, the required profile in a national crisis (such as a war, or economic crisis) may be significantly different to that in a time of peace and prosperity. To illustrate this in a UK context, during World War II the leader of the UK needed to be extremely high on:

- Emotional resilience
- Influence
- Intuitiveness
- Motivation

There can be little doubt that Winston Churchill exhibited all these elements. However, it is important to bear in mind that these elements are not only required in a crisis. They are **enduring** elements which assume different significance in crisis situations.

In the totally different context of the early 2000s with the UK enjoying a period of relative economic affluence and stability, but recovering from a bruising transformation of business life and exposure to business and governmental 'scandals' the elements of emotional intelligence at a premium are:

- Self-awareness

- Conscientiousness

- Interpersonal sensitivity

- Motivation (new goals)

- Emotional resilience (adhering to economic disciplines)

Again there is little doubt that the current Prime Minister Tony Blair appears to exhibit these elements of emotional intelligence.

While we can dispute these national (and UK-biased) examples we can all think of more concrete examples related to the leadership of our own organisations. However, whether operating at the national (and theoretical) level or more specific (and practical) level we can also recognise specific situations in which the dominant requirements are offset by the lesser requirements. Although there will be differing priorities on the elements of emotional intelligence, in all cases a **balance** is needed. For example, Winston Churchill may have faced situations as a leader in which he needed to display interpersonal sensitivity within an overall context which did not place a premium on this. Similarly, Tony Blair has faced situations in which he has needed to display intuitiveness even though not a priority in the overall context.

What we do seem to know about emotional intelligence is that, given an average level of IQ it predicts success in terms of advancement in an organisation. Thus it would seem that emotionally intelligent leaders should be able to lead organisations through periods of significant or transformational change. While the evidence for this relationship is only just beginning to emerge in academic terms, what we do know from experience is that organisations which have been successful in achieving significant transformation have leaders who exhibit different qualities from those associated with successful **management** of stable organisations. Furthermore, such leaders have been successful in transforming the behaviours of large numbers of key players within their organisations. Thus leadership in these situations is a 'team' rather than a 'solo' game. The top individual leaders have not only demonstrated significant personal levels of emotional intelligence but also encouraged or released the emotional intelligence of other leaders within their organisations.

The importance of the dynamic between the leadership requirement and the leadership context has been highlighted in this chapter. In the next two chapters we will consider the team and the relationship between the organisation, its culture and the promotion or nurturing of emotional intelligence within the organisation.

Teams and Emotional Intelligence

So far, we have concentrated on the EIQ (which in this chapter is reflected in the EIQ measure) of the *individual* and, having described the seven elements, have produced a model which describes how these disparate characteristics relate to each other, and how a degree of balance is so important. What are the implications for group working, something which is so critical nowadays in leaner, flatter companies and other situations where teamwork is required?

There has probably been more research conducted by occupational psychologists into groups than into any other topic, with the possible exception of leadership. Most of this has identified the totally independent dimensions of group work – those activities related to the task, and its achievement; and those related to the interpersonal relationships (the people aspects) sometimes referred to as 'process' factors. A semantic complication has been the interchangeability of the words group and team, without any clear definition given. In our view, a team is a group, but with additional characteristics:

- all members share common aims
- all members share responsibility for outcomes
- all members are highly committed to achieving common objectives and high-quality results
- the members are interdependent
- individual success equates to group success

In short, the whole is greater than the sum of the parts.

The most celebrated work on management teams was conducted by Dr Meredith Belbin and colleagues over a ten-year period at Henley Management College. They studied literally hundreds of syndicates (teams) working on a business simulation exercise in which they ran their companies over a simulated three-year period, all competing with similar products in the same market. Not only did the researchers have the results of the business performance of each team; they also had personality profiles and mental ability test results, and detailed behavioural records of how each member of each team had actually performed throughout the week-long exercise.

After thorough analysis of the composition and behaviour of both high and low performing teams, a number of 'team roles' were identified. These constitute clusters of related behaviours which some managers demonstrated by dint of their personality and intellectual ability. The team roles covered not only the task and people dimensions, but added a third – ideas. In other words, a team role is a preference or predisposition to behave in a certain way over a period of time. Eight different team roles were identified:

Plant: The creative, ideas person

Resource Investigator: The networker and entrepreneur

Co-ordinator: The participative leader

Shaper: The driving, up-front leader

Monitor Evaluator: The intelligent, analytical critic

Team Worker: The people-oriented facilitator

Implementer: The task implementation person

Completer Finisher: The quality-assurer and time-keeper.

More detailed descriptions of each role's positive characteristics and personality factors, and allowable weaknesses, are presented in **Table 9.1.**

Table 9.1: Team Role Definitions and Related Personality Descriptors

Roles and Descriptions Team Role Contributions	Allowable Weaknesses	Personality Factors	
Plant (PL): Creative, imaginative, unorthodox. Solves difficult problems.	Weak in communication with and managing ordinary people.	Assertive Venturesome Detached Forthright Serious	Experimenting Tender minded Intelligent Imaginative Self-sufficient
Resource Investigator (RI): Extrovert, enthusiastic, communicative. Explores opportunities. Develops contacts.	Loses interest once initial enthusiasm has passed.	Calm Venturesome Imaginative	Radical Trusting
Co-ordinator (CO): Mature, confident and trusting. A good chairman. Clarifies goals, promotes decision-making.	Not necessarily the most clever or creative member of a group.	Calm Assertive Trusting Enthusiastic	Detached Practical Conscientious Controlled
Shaper (SH): Dynamic, outgoing, highly strung. Challenges, pressurises, finds way round obstacles.	Prone to provocation and short-lived bursts of temper.	Tense Anxious Assertive Venturesome	Expedient Tough-minded Suspicious Apprehensive
Monitor Evaluator (ME): Sober, strategic and discerning. Sees all options. Judges accurately	Lacks drive and ability to inspire others.	Intelligent Serious-minded	Shrewd
Team Worker (TW): Social, mild, perceptive and accommodating. Listens, builds, averts friction.	Indecisive in crunch situations.	Outgoing Trusting	Unassertive Group-oriented
Implementer (IM): Disciplined, reliable, conservative and efficient. Turns ideas into practical actions.	Somewhat inflexible, slow to respond to new possibilities.	Conscientious Tough-minded Practical	Trusting Conservative Controlled
Completer Finisher (CF): Painstaking, conscientious, anxious. Searches out errors and omissions. Delivers on time.	Inclined to worry unduly. Reluctant to delegate.	Anxious Tense Controlled	Conscientious Apprehensive

Belbin's original work, and many other research and case-studies conducted subsequently, have shown that management teams in which all eight roles are filled by at least one person perform at a much higher level, in a wider range of different tasks, than other less well 'balanced' teams. An important caveat is that there should, ideally, not be more than one shaper, and not too many plants in a team, otherwise there is likely to be friction and division in the former case, and too much talking and not enough action in the latter. Belbin's 'theory' is now extremely well established, and widely used around the world. It has also been copied by many other management academics and consultants, endorsing the recognition of its usefulness. Recent research, in particular that of Terri Hunter, has demonstrated that the theory 'works' with junior management and non-management teams. A key word in describing the theory is 'balance'. A team of different individuals, each with a distinctive set of strengths and allowable weaknesses, is likely to perform better than a team of, for example, highly bright and dynamic 'superstars', all of whom are from the same mould.

'Balance' is also a critical feature of our model of emotional intelligence, described in **chapter 5**. So, are there common principles between Belbin's theory of teams and our model of EQ which can be used to build better teams? We believe there are, and the results from our own study of managers (see **chapter 3**) provided us with some pointers. Since we had personality profiles for our entire sample, we were able to calculate each person's team roles. Several distinct similarities emerged between specific Belbin Team Roles (TRs) and the elements of EQ, within the framework of our model, with its three main features.

Drivers
> Two TRs seemed to fit neatly into this category. Those with **high** EQ motivation are likely to play the **shaper** role, and to drive the team to achieving goals, and ultimately to success. In addition, the **resource investigator**, being highly energetic and enthusiastic, is usually very effective at motivating fellow team members, and spotting opportunities for the team to exploit. (The **resource investigator** also probably fits under the enablers.)

Constrainers

One TR has links with these EQ characteristics. The **completer finisher**, being a perfectionist, the person preoccupied with quality and timing, is likely to possess the EQ qualities of conscientiousness, and will therefore apply these characteristics to good effect. He or she will probably curb the excesses of expedient colleagues and demand high standards of output from colleagues, and will probably bring the team back on track whenever it is behind time. Much time can be saved by exposing and rejecting flawed ideas at an early stage.

Personal and Inter-Personal Enablers

The enablers embrace not only the EQ elements of influence, self-awareness and sensitivity, but also 'IQ', intellectual competencies, and 'MQ' management competencies. Those with high influence, self-awareness and sensitivity, and with high MQ, especially appraising and developing staff and communication, are probably fitted to play the **co-ordinator** role very effectively, in terms of leading the team in a democratic, participative, 'hands-off' style. In contrast, those with just the three EQ elements are likely to be well fitted to the purely people-focused **team worker** role, the person who will concentrate on building group cohesiveness, encourage communications between members and reduce conflict and disharmony. Those who are highly conscientious and practical are the ones who would make good **implementers**, those who have a 'hands-on' role in implementing any action plans designed by colleagues. Those individuals who score highly on EQ intuitiveness, and who also have high IQ (an enabler), are probably suited to the **monitor evaluator** role. Finally, the sensitive members with high IQ and a creative streak are the ones who would most probably play the **plant** role, the member who generates all the creative ideas and proposals.

We have already mentioned that those who are highly enthusiastic and who in turn motivate colleagues have many of the **resource investigator** characteristics. This role however could also be seen as an 'enabling' role, especially for those individuals who score highly on EQ influence (good for networking and exploiting opportunities) and who also have high MQ, in particular good communication skills and business sense. These are the team members who will create business opportunities and win new customers for the team.

A summary of the links between EQ elements and team roles is presented in **Figure 9.1.** This demonstrates the potential for using the EQ model on a team basis, for bringing together individuals whose own EQ scores may not be in balance, but who nevertheless collectively complement each others' strengths and allowable weaknesses, to improve team cohesion and performance.

We can all think of teams who perform badly because they are not well balanced, and because members do not complement each other. There are many football or cricket teams which spring to mind, but let us take a look at two examples of dysfunctional work teams where EI is out of balance. First, consider a sales team, with members all from the same mould. They all score highly on the enablers – they are very persuasive and good at influencing other people; and they are responsive and sensitive to the needs and feelings of other people. They are also very high on motivation – they are enthusiastic, dynamic, energetic individuals, who are all driven to succeed, and to attain high targets. To do so they are very decisive people, who make decisions on the spur of the moment, based upon their intuition and 'gut-feel'. In contrast, however, they have a low level of awareness of their own feelings and emotions, and are unable to handle them effectively. Importantly, they are not very conscientious and have a low level of integrity. What are the consequences of this unbalanced EI team likely to be? It will most probably produce a very exhilarating and enjoyable atmosphere, with a lot of energy and enthusiasm demonstrated, and a constant buzz of excitement and expectation. Individuals are likely to create a highly sociable

Figure 9.1: Team EQ and Team Roles

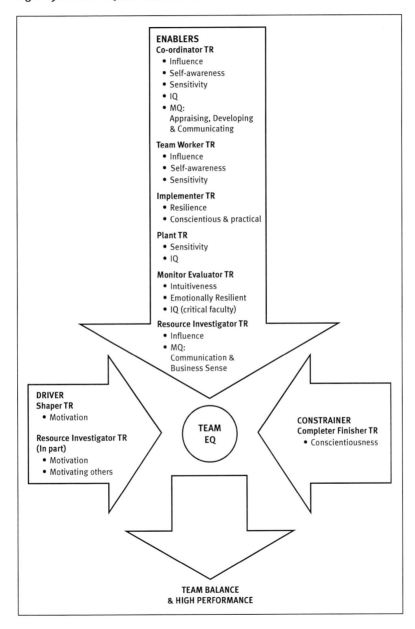

atmosphere, with an emphasis not only on achieving targets but also on having fun. However, because none of the team members are high on the EI Constrainers, everyone is likely to cut corners and to show a lack of concern about meeting deadlines, or about the quality of the service or product being offered. All of them are likely to bend, if not break the rules if it helps to achieve results, and some may even transgress the law. When performance falls or problems occur, as they inevitably will, with low resilience will come friction and disharmony within the team, caused by an inability of all members to control their feelings and disappointments. More often than not, this results in a downward spiral of performance which is very difficult to arrest.

Another type of dysfunctional team is where many or all members have high enablers but, in contrast to the first team, motivation is low and the conscientiousness of all members is very high. This team is preoccupied with the detail and with getting everything just right. Everything has to be done by the book. There will also be a preoccupation with the quality of the output, even if it takes three times as long to achieve that final five per cent of quality. Members lack intuitiveness and spend forever seeking more and more information before being willing to take a decision. They also lack energy and motivation, and sometimes run out of steam before they complete the task. With a lack of urgency and purpose things are readily put off until tomorrow. In such a team there is also a predisposition to concentrate on the short-term tasks and to forget about the long-term objectives or final output. The atmosphere is unlikely to be stimulating or exciting, and there is likely to be a preoccupation with one's own feelings, and the feelings of other members. This in turn can lead to a preoccupation with how the team is working and why the members are not feeling fulfilled, to the detriment of task achievement, the ultimate purpose of a work team. We can all think of times when we have been on the receiving end of such teams.

So what would constitute a high performing EI team? First, not everyone has to have high scores on all seven elements of EI. A fairly balanced set of scores within an individual's profile would be desirable – it would be unrealistic to expect that all members of a team had high scores on all elements, plus high intelligence (IQ) and MQ as well. Indeed, a team of superstars would probably not work well together and would demonstrate conflict and disharmony. The requirement for a successful EI team is:

- At least one or two members who have very high motivation

- One or two members who are conscientious and who possess high levels of conscientiousness and integrity

- Most, if not all, members who have average or above scores on the enablers – self-awareness, resilience, influence, intuitiveness and interpersonal sensitivity.

It would also be beneficial for the team to contain at least one or two members with high IQ and high MQ – the management competencies of business sense, communication skills and staff-management skills.

In such a team the drivers would be kept in check by those who were conscientious and who had high ethical standards. Some would concentrate on producing and evaluating ideas. Some would focus on influencing people and getting new business and achieving results and others could focus on organisation and team working. There would be a positive and exciting atmosphere, in which debate and argument would thrive, but would be handled maturely and productively. Members would gravitate to those tasks which fitted their preferences and abilities, and the whole would be more than the sum of its parts – the essence of effective team work.

In those instances where it is not possible for management to conduct a Team Role analysis on their staff because the psychometric personality data are not available, our research to date suggests that it could well be advantageous to analyse the EQ profiles of each member, in order to explore the overall EQ balance of the team, in terms of drivers, constrainers and enablers. As with the Belbin analysis, if the team is deficient in certain areas, and since we believe that EQ elements can be developed or exploited, special development action should be considered in cases where individuals currently have an average score. If, however, there are gaps which no-one in the team is likely to be able to fill, even with development, then this suggests that management might have to revert to the 'transfer market', to bring in new talent.

We noted in **chapter 3** that the EQ elements reflect a wide range of personality characteristics covering four of the five main dimensions of adult personality. In this chapter we have extended the EQ model, from the individual to the group level of analysis, and have commented on the similarities between EQ and Belbin Team Roles. We have also suggested that there is scope for using EQ assessments to help in building balanced, and therefore effective and flexible teams. In the next chapter we take our analysis up yet another level, to look at EQ and the total organisation, and in particular how the organisation's culture affects the EQ of individuals, and teams working within it.

Emotional Intelligence and Organisations

Introduction

For much of the 20th century the predominant thinking about organisations was strongly influenced by the sociologist Max Weber. Weber proposed the idea of practical rationality which encompassed:

- Rational technique: the calculated use of means

- Technical rationality: the progress from technique to the use of more effective means

- Rational choice of ends (on the basis of knowledge and precise calculation)

- Life-guiding principles: action guided by generalised value principles

- Rational-methodology lifestyle: the unification and balance of the above points to ensure their joint success.

He highlighted these points as a counterbalance to 'emotionality' which he saw as an integral and significant aspect of behaviour in an organisational context. Thus he saw bureaucracy as a way to organisational control and a means of legitimising authority. Weber is often portrayed as the 'father' of rationality. However, he was far from disinterested in the 'emotional' aspects of organisations and was particularly interested in affectivity as one of his four types of social actions. It is often proposed that Weber discounted emotions within his bureaucratic model. However, he did allow for emotion with bureaucracy, albeit that their rational understanding should become an intrinsic part of their working. Indeed his work was designed to explore the dialectic between rationality and affectivity. To simplify the Weberian 'philosophy' the emphasis on rationality is concerned with rationalisation of both the instrumental and emotional aspects of organisation behaviour.

The translation of Weberian principles into managerial frameworks was epitomised by Taylor and his views on scientific management. This highly rational model provided the foundation of the production line approach to processes which both influenced practitioners and writers on management well into the 1950s. Arguably the inheritance of this thinking has been seen in the way in which organisations worked well into the 1970s. It was perhaps not until the Total Quality Movement (TQM) became significant that the fundamental principles of Taylorism were challenged.

In this obsession with rationality in organisation and process design, the historical origins of Weber's work have been observed. Weber's call for rationality was underpinned by earlier concerns about the abuse of collective power voiced by influential writers in the period of the industrial revolution. Thus the purpose (i.e. prevention of abuse of power) has been eclipsed by the process (i.e. the focus on bureaucracy as a means of ensuring rationality). This focus reinforces Weber's nightmare of the 'disenchantment of the world'. This fundamental point has been resurrected in the field of sociology by writers such as Albrow. In a recent book Albrow presented a collection of papers which addressed the topic of emotion in organisations and highlighted the importance of working with both the rational and emotional elements of behaviour in an organisational context.

While these developments have been taking place in the sociological arena, parallel developments have been taking place in the field of management and organisational behaviour. In the more popular and pragmatic world of business we have seen, in the last five years or so, a focus on 'people as a competitive advantage' and associated views and models relating to how we might develop and exploit this 'resource'. A stream of writing has been associated with this trend which has begun to examine the way in which emotion has been a neglected area when building approaches to developing managers and leaders. This growing emergence of thinking has tended to lead to a fundamental challenge to the Cartesian conception of rationality which has dominated our education and opened our minds to new paradigms. Typical of this emerging stream of thinking is the book, edited by Steve Fineman, on *Emotion in Organisations* which explores alternative ways of construing rationality.

To a large extent the challenges faced by organisations in operating in a complex, highly volatile, competitive and global environment have been shown to be inadequately addressed by the 'rational model' (and its many adaptations). This failure of the established ways of thinking about organisations has led to a growing focus on the non-rational aspects of organisation behaviour such as vision, mission and values, rather than the traditional rational focus on strategy, goals and objectives. Indeed the approaches to core strategy formulation have shifted from an exclusively analytical approach to the more intuitive and 'emotive' approach in the resource-based view of strategy. The links between such a shift in thinking and organisational success were highlighted in the book *Built to Last*, by Collins and Porras. In their work Collins and Porras pointed to many drivers of corporate success which can be seen as being more readily associated with the 'emotional' than the 'rational' elements of the organisation. Typical of such claims are that the evidence demonstrates that the consistently successful organisations have a 'Purpose beyond profit' and set 'Big, Hairy, Audacious Goals' (BHAGs). This is not the language of the analytical strategists and corporate planners. Yet it has clearly resonated with the practical experience of many leaders and is seen as offering a viable and, potentially more exciting, alternative to the failed volumes of strategy documents which seem incapable of implementation. The number of organisational executives who readily converse in terms of purpose, vision and even BHAGs is a testament to this shift in thinking. However, it is evident that organisational success does not result from the 'emotional' route alone (any more than, in reality, it did from the 'rational' route alone). The key to success appears to lie in achieving a balance between the emotional and rational strands of organisational thinking and behaviour. This need for balance is summarised in **Figure 10.1**. Reviewing this diagram illustrates that strategy has two components which lead down differing implementation routes. Most leading thinkers and writers on strategy emphasise that implementation is critical to success. With the 'new' model it is clear that organisations need to be focused on both achieving results and aligning individual behaviours with their goals and strategy.

Relationship to Emotional Intelligence

Reviewing the arguments developed above will give rise to a recognition that there are clear parallels between these, at an organisational level, and the arguments for the significance of emotional intelligence outlined in the earlier chapters of this book. Indeed much of the enthusiasm with which organisations have greeted the concept of emotional intelligence may be seen to be a result of the new thinking in terms of drivers of corporate success. However, the very enthusiasm with which emotional intelligence has been greeted in so many settings may be seen as its ability to explain individual performance and contribution – vital to corporate success, but evidently in short supply! Reflecting on the above leads us to raise two distinct, but related, questions which are:

- How do organisations encourage or develop the emotional intelligence of their people?
- Can organisations be emotionally intelligent?

The first of these questions may be seen as being related to the extent to which the culture of the organisation recognises, nurtures and promotes (in the broadest as well as specific sense) individuals who display elements of emotional intelligence. Conversely do some organisational cultures destroy or punish the exhibition of elements of emotional intelligence by its people?

Figure 10.1: Balancing the Emotional and Rational Aspects

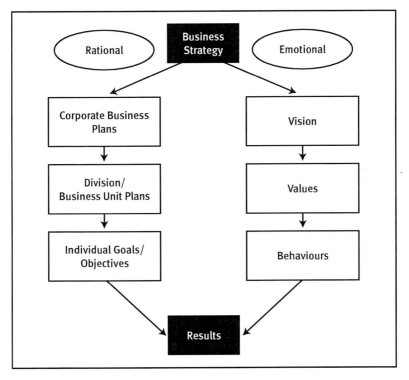

The second question relates to the extent to which it may be possible to exhibit organisational equivalents of the components of emotional intelligence. If so, how may these be developed at an organisational level?

These two questions are explored in more detail in the remainder of this chapter. It is important to point out that, while our work on individual emotional intelligence has been rooted in structured empirical research, our proposals in this chapter are based on practical experiences, anecdotal examples and intuitive speculation (combined with some initial exploratory reseach). However, at this point in the book we sincerely hope that the reader has bought into the value of intuition in dealing with incomplete or ambiguous information!

Organisation Culture and Emotional Intelligence

The first question raised above takes us into the field of organisational culture. This is an extremely difficult area riddled with definitional and philosophical debate. It is exceedingly difficult to define exactly what is meant by organisational culture but, this is at odds with our everyday experience. Most of us are able to recognise the distinct characteristics or 'feel' of the organisations in which we work or those that we deal with on a regular basis. These distinctive components are more closely related to the specific organisation than the business sector in which it operates. For the purposes of this chapter we are less concerned with definitional niceties than we are with organisational realities. For our exploration we are proud to borrow the definition of organisational culture employed by the Chief Executive of a financial services organisation with which we worked. 'Culture is about the way we do things around here.' (In turn we believe that he borrowed this from Edgar Schein!)

While we may applaud the insight and pragmatism of this statement it is necessary to have a more structured framework with which to explore our question. The framework presented in a book by Rob Goffee of London Business School and Gareth Jones, formerly of Henley Management College (*The Character of a Corporation*) seems to present an extremely useful one within which we might explore our first question. Goffee and Jones explain that their framework relates to the social architecture of an organisation. From our perspective this provided a valuable link to our starting point in this chapter. The social architecture of an organisation is influenced both by the perspective of the nature of organisations itself and also by the specific organisational evolution of their interpretation of this perspective in pursuit of their business goals. In addition, the Goffee and Jones model is appealing as it encompasses the following contextual elements:

(a) There is no 'right' culture *per se*, only a culture which is appropriate to the business requirement.

(b) Within an organisation differing cultures co-exist. They can do this effectively if each is appropriate to the respective needs of the business units, divisions or functions.

(c) Culture is not fixed; it changes over time and, indeed, may be seen as following a life cycle.

(d) While each cultural 'type' within the framework is valid in relation to specific business contexts, each can exist in a way which is positive and supportive or negative and damaging.

Having focused on the reasons for choosing the Goffee and Jones framework to explore our argument it is important to explain the nature of their cultural model. In essence they demonstrate that the social architecture of an organisation may be seen in terms of two dimensions: sociability and solidarity. These dimensions are described in broad terms as follows:

Sociability

According to Goffee and Jones, sociability is about the level of friendliness among members of a community. It is to do with the extent to which relationships are valued for their own sake and the extent to which people within the community relate to each other in a friendly, caring, way. Sociability is also impacted by the extent to which members of the community have shared values, views and ideas. This concept can be applied within business organisations as much as other communities. In an organisational context, sociability is also reflected in the degree of social links between the working and personal lives of the members of the organisation.

To an extent sociability displays a degree of persistency over time. Relationships which I form with others in my organisation are not instrumental (i.e. focused on results only) and relate to affectivity rather than results.

Solidarity

Goffee and Jones describe solidarity in terms of the extent to which there is commonality of tasks and a clear understanding of mutual interests. In a business context, solidarity is concerned with the extent to which members of the organisation have a clear and shared vision and related goals which are independent of the extent to which members like each other. The focus in high solidarity organisations tends to be on results; there are clear goals, performance measures and a clear competitive strategy.

Unlike sociability the solidarity dimension is more transient. Solidarity is contingent upon organisational goals and more intermittent. While the relationships in the sociability scale transcend changes in the organisational context, solidarity interactions do not. For example, today I work with you closely because the interaction between our two functions is crucial to achieving organisational goals. Tomorrow those goals change and our interaction no longer has any relevance. Thus, in solidarity terms, I no longer need to interact with you. This does not change my personal views about you as an individual. However, it does change the utility of our interaction in pursuit of core business goals.

In addition to defining the two dimensions Goffee and Jones point out that the resulting culture may be positive, in the sense of being appropriate for the business, or negative in terms of inhibiting the effective achievement of business goals. In addition, they highlight that there is no 'best' culture, only one which is appropriate for the needs of the business. The combination of these dimensions results in an overall model which is illustrated in **Figure 10.2**.

The four cultures emerging from this model may be summarised as follows:

Networked Culture

The Networked Culture is one in which the level of sociability is high and the level of solidarity is relatively low. Thus it is a culture within which relationships are perceived as being more important than concentration on tasks and goals. Typically it is a culture in which results are achieved by tapping into and leveraging the relationship network.

Figure 10.2: Double S Cube Model

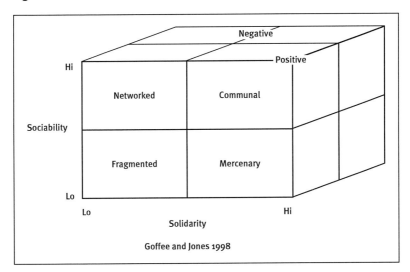

Goffee and Jones 1998

Communal Culture

In an organisation with a communal culture there are high levels of both sociability and solidarity. Both relationships and tasks/goals are very important. Such a culture is typical of 'start up' operations where the founders and early employees are a community who value their relationships and are committed to a clear vision and goals for the business.

Mercenary Culture

The Mercenary Culture has an over-riding task and performance culture. Organisations with such a culture could be seen as being the corporate equivalent of 'driven' individuals. The focus is on winning; beating the competition.

Fragmented Culture

The fragmented culture is about the value to the business of individuality. Little is shared. Relationships are relatively unimportant and there is a low level of focus on shared goals and commitment to beating the competition. While this sounds negative, it can be appropriate for organisations which achieve performance by providing maximum freedom for individual innovation and are able to find opportunities to leverage such contribution. For example a number of professional services firms operate successfully with such 'light' culture.

It is beyond the scope of this chapter to describe the Goffee and Jones model in detail (indeed the best way to access the detail is to read their own work). However, for the purposes of developing our ideas about the relationship between emotional intelligence and organisational culture it will be helpful to understand some of the positive and negative aspects of each of the four cultural typologies. These are summarised in **Table 10.1** below.

Table 10.1: Positive and Negative Aspects of the Cultural Typologies

Networked	
Positively networked	**Negatively networked**
Informality	Gossip, rumour
Flexibility	'Negative' politics
Rapid exchange of information	Endless debate about measures
Willingness to help	Long meetings with no action
High trust	Manipulation of communication, e.g. copying e-mails
Ease of communication – no hidden agendas	'Cover Your Ass' management style
Fun, laughter	Risk aversion – 'keep your head down'
Loyalty	Change jobs in the organisation frequently (this builds networks and minimises performance measurement)
Empathy	

Caring for others	Concentrate more on managing upwards than managing outcomes
Compatible people	
Less defensiveness	
Relaxed	

Mercenary	
Positively mercenary	**Negatively mercenary**
Focused	Internally competitive – no time for co-operation
High energy task oriented	Only does what is measured
Energy	Poor at alliance management (because alliances always require the management of ambiguity and mercenary cultures are bad at this)
High levels of competition awareness	
Recognition of shared interests	Fails to explore synergy opportunities (good at exploiting them once they are clear)
Quick response rate	
Intolerance of poor performance	Fragile psychological contract (this is a real problem in businesses where knowledge management is critical, e.g. pharmaceutical industry)
Conflicts openly addressed	
	'Quick suicide' – will march over the cliff in step – intolerance of dissent
Relentless pursuit of improving measured outcomes and standards	

Fragmented	
Positively fragmented	**Negatively fragmented**
Freedom from org. interference	Selfish
Focus on individual excellence	No knowledge sharing (secretive)
Set out own agenda	Low identification with organisation
Define your own goals	Very fragile psychological contract
Scope for individual creativity	Cannot manage meetings or any collective events
Work with who you choose (either inside or outside) (therefore good opportunities to network)	Bad mouth colleagues (excessive critique can degenerate into inaction)
Can steal ideas and practices from anywhere	ALL ideas get savaged
Resources follow 'stars' (i.e. those who can deliver get what they need)	
Space to explore ideas without either sociability or solidarity getting in the way	
Communal	
Positively communal	**Negatively communal**
Passionate	Sense of invulnerability
Committed	Inability to see strengths of competitors
High energy	No leadership development, only disciples
Creative	Excessive reliance on charismatic founder figures

Communal *continued*	
Positively communal	**Negatively communal**
Able to sustain teams over long periods	Willingness to 'carry' under-achieving colleagues, as long as they continue to believe in the values, that is to say confusing beliefs with performance
Loyal	
Equitable, fair, just	Unwillingness to change
Close tie between espoused values and embedded practices stimul-ating (rather more than fun – almost obsessive)	

Reflecting on this model it is possible to hypothesise that some of these cultures would be more likely than others to nurture and promote emotional intelligence. **Figure 10.3** illustrates the likely relationship between the organisation culture and emotional intelligence.

Figure 10.3: Organisational Culture and Emotional Intelligence

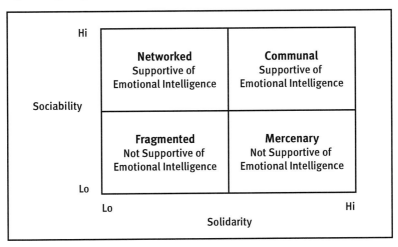

Although the two dimensions provide a useful framework it is important to emphasise the appropriateness of culture. Goffee and Jones are now proposing that cultural appropriateness is related to the underlying strategic variables facing the business. This relationship is, somewhat simplistically, summarised in **Figure 10.4**.

Figure 10.4: Culture and Strategic Variables

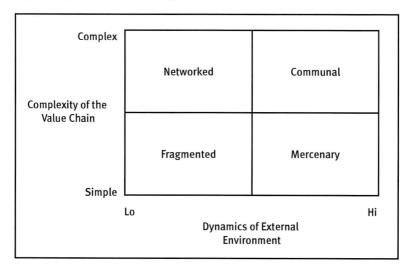

This view of the relationship between organisational culture is somewhat simplistic. However, it is clear that the mercenary culture will be one in which there is a greater concern over the achievement of results than the interpersonal behaviours employed in arriving at goals. In a fragmented culture, relationships are incidental and not particularly valued. Thus in both of these cultures the environment will not be conducive to the development of the abilities which lead to high emotional intelligence. This can lead to both voluntary and involuntary loss of employees and potentially low morale. This would particularly be so if the culture were misaligned with the business requirements (i.e. negative mercenary or negative fragmented). In the high sociability cultures (networked and communal) the value placed on relationships is such that the behaviours associated with high emotional intelligence are likely to be endorsed and rewarded.

Looking at the cultural relationship with emotional intelligence is a useful point from which to explore the particular aspects or elements of emotional intelligence which are described in **chapter 3**. Indeed the model which we described in **chapter 5** provides us with a means of developing a more meaningful understanding of the relationship. For example within a mercenary culture, not all elements of emotional intelligence would be unrewarded. It is likely that, in such a culture, the components of decisiveness would be highly valued and promoted. Influence could also play a role in terms of upward influence of those in clear power positions. However, the high results focus of the culture could well lead to an 'ends justify the means' mind-set with resulting expediency in decision-making and action. This would tend to lead to a low valuing and nurturing of the component conscientiousness. Using this approach to analysing the relationship between culture and the elements of emotional intelligence enables us to expand the model shown in **Figure 10.3** and develop a more useful framework. **Table 10.2** summarises these expanded relationships.

From **Table 10.2** we can see (using the driver, constrainer, enabler model) that:

- Networked cultures tend to support the enablers in the main, but discourage (or are neutral in relation to) the drivers.

- Communal organisations tend to value and promote a mixture of enablers, drivers and constrainers. They are unlikely to 'punish' exhibition of any of the components of emotional intelligence. In this sense they can be viewed as offering an environment which is broadly supportive of not only specific components but the balance which is the hallmark of high emotional intelligence.

- Mercenary cultures are likely to primarily support the drivers of emotional intelligence and, to an extent the enablers. However, they tend to inhibit the constrainers.

- Fragmented cultures are more focused in their potential support for the drivers. Like the mercenary organisations they will be likely to inhibit the constrainers. However, they are more likely than mercenary cultures to also inhibit the development of the enablers.

Table 10.2: Culture and Components of Emotional Intelligence

Culture	EI Components		
	Likely to be Rewarded/Supported	Likely to be 'Punished'	Neutral
Networked	• Interpersonal Sensitivity • Conscientiousness • Influence • Self-awareness	• Motivation	• Intuitiveness • Emotional Resilience
Communal	• Self-awareness • Conscientiousness • Interpersonal Sensitivity • Intuitiveness • Influence		• Motivation • Emotional Resilience
Mercenary	• Motivation • Emotional Resilience • Intuitiveness • Influence	• Interpersonal Sensitivity • Conscientiousness • Self-awareness	
Fragmented	• Intuitiveness • Motivation	• Conscientiousness • Interpersonal Sensitivity • Self-awareness	• Emotional Resilience • Influence

We have worked with a relatively simple view of the Goffee and Jones model. In practice, they identify that even when an organisation's culture is appropriate for its business context, the culture may exist in either a positive or negative form. In order to fully explore the relationships between culture and emotional intelligence in the longer term, we need to consider both appropriateness and the positive or negative format of the culture. For example, in **Table 10.2** we have shown that in a networked culture conscientiousness is likely to be rewarded or supported. This attribution assumes a **positive** networked culture. This additional dimension of culture has significant implications for the development and nurturing of emotional intelligence.

Implications of the Cultural Impact on Emotional Intelligence

At this stage in our understanding of the relationship between organisational cultures and emotional intelligence it would be somewhat rash to be prescriptive in suggesting how organisations might react to an analysis such as has been presented above. However, two potential reactions might be considered. These are:

- Ensure that selection processes highlight the 'compatible and incompatible' elements of an individual's emotional intelligence. Such data could either be used to screen out potential mismatches, or be used in an open discussion of realistic opportunities and challenges which might be faced by an individual who is 'mismatched' with the culture in this respect. While this approach may result in a loss of otherwise well-matched candidates, it could help to avoid the difficulties of losing people who find the cultural mismatch too uncomfortable and the potential of damage to morale of having such people remain in the organisation.

- Review the 'people systems' to identify potential areas for change which could reduce the EI punishing impact of the culture. This reaction, while potentially having a long-term impact on the nature of the culture may be attainable in a way which significant or fundamental culture change could not.

If the organisation is completely comfortable with the fit between its culture and its business requirements, the first of these options may be the more appropriate. If there is any sense that the culture may need to change in the mid- to long-term, or that there are undesirable negative elements of the culture present, the second option could be useful.

Consideration of the impact of 'people' systems and processes on the support for and development of the emotional intelligence of individuals is likely to entail examination of the following areas:

Reward systems

Are results the only drivers of reward decisions? Would it be possible to include behaviours or 'softer' objectives (e.g. levels of employee satisfaction) in the reward decision criteria without damaging the business objectives being supported by the current system?

Promotion systems

Do the current promotion systems include criteria which reflect elements of emotional intelligence? Could the criteria be extended to include such elements (or more of them) without damage to the goals and success criteria of the system?

Competency frameworks

If competency frameworks are employed within the organisation do they include the components of emotional intelligence? If not, could these be added in a practical way without diluting the focus and purposes of the framework?

Training and development systems

Are any of the elements of emotional intelligence dealt with on company training programmes? If not, could they be included or covered in separate programmes? Do developmental processes (e.g. needs analysis, coaching, etc.) focus on behaviours as well as business/technical/professional topics? If not could a shift in focus be effected in a practical way?

Performance appraisal

Does the performance appraisal system encompass reviews of behaviours as well as results? If not, could the behavioural elements be included without detracting from the business goals of the organisation?

Working with these thoughts, we carried out a highly exploratory study with 16 organisations to examine the relationships between the average level of emotional intelligence of employees and ratings of the organisation using simple scales to explore 'cultural' dimensions. This study produced indications that there was a relationship between these dimensions and average level of employee emotional intelligence. This result prompted us to develop the idea further. Using the study results, together with a detailed review of the literature on organisational culture we developed a more structured cultural assessment questionnaire (the Emotional Intelligence Cultural Audit, or EICA).

The questionnaire contains 113 items that are rated using a Likert scale in the same manner as the EIQ: M. The statements in the EICA refer to the behaviours and processes that are observable within the organisation and which represent manifestations of the culture of an organisation. For example:

In performance appraisal discussions behaviours and results are given equal weight.

The questionnaire was developed to be completed by multiple respondents and to produce seven culture clusters designed to indicate the extent to which cultural manifestations support the individual elements of EI. The conceptualisation of the seven EI culture elements is summarised in **Figure 10.5**.

While the above list and description of subsequent research is by no means exhaustive, hopefully they provide some food for thought and may prompt the reader to identify other 'people' systems and processes which could be reviewed in their organisation. Although not wishing to generate further lists to consider, we should point out that we chose the term 'people systems and processes' quite deliberately. The review process can go beyond the traditional HR or personnel processes. For example, the way in which meetings are organised and conducted can impact both positively and negatively on the support for and nurturing of emotional intelligence. In any review within your own organisation it will be valuable to take a broad view of what you include in your interpretation of 'people systems and processes'.

Achieving a change in systems and processes intended to enhance the climate for the development of emotional intelligence will take time and sustained effort. However, this mirrors, at an organisational level, the observation we made in **chapter 7** that developing individual emotional intelligence takes time. For both individuals and organisations there are no 'quick fixes'.

Can Organisations be Emotionally Intelligent?

In the preceding sections of this chapter we focused on the way in which organisational culture impacts on the climate in which individual emotional intelligence is exercised and developed. We now turn to the second question which we raised at the beginning of the chapter – can organisations be emotionally intelligent? While one aspect of an emotionally intelligent organisation would be the creation of a climate which fosters the development of individual emotional intelligence, we suggest that the idea of an emotionally intelligent organisation is broader than this.

The resource based view of strategy entails consideration of organisational competencies or capabilities. Our starting point for the examination of individual emotional intelligence was individual competencies. The seven components of emotional intelligence are, in themselves, competency based. There would seem to be a logic which lends some support, through a competency argument, for the concept of organisational emotional intelligence. A way of developing a picture of what an emotionally intelligent organisation might be like is to identify the organisation level equivalents of the seven components of emotional intelligence. Our proposed organisational components are shown in **Figure 10.5** below

Figure 10.5: Emotional Intelligence Culture Element Descriptors

---

Self Awareness

The organisation has processes in place which make it aware of how it feels about its business, products, markets and stakeholders at any time. This awareness is based on a clear self-image which is widely shared within the organisation. It is aware of how these feelings impact on its decisions and behaviours. It is aware of how stakeholders and other outsiders perceive the organisation and its actions.

Emotional Resilience

The organisation has processes in place which enable it to absorb attack and criticism (particularly if it is perceived as unfair or unjust). It is able to manage internal communications in a way which ensures that such attacks do not deflect it from its strategy. It recognises potentially damaging shifts in its internal climate and has systems for controlling and managing these.

Motivation

There are clear, well understood and shared long-term goals. Events, which appear to threaten or deflect performance, are responded to in a way that ensures that the long-term strategy remains intact. Actions that are short term are avoided if their benefits will damage achievement of long-term aims. Business setbacks are seen as problems to be managed rather than leading to the abandonment of long-term goals.

Interpersonal Sensitivity
The organisation has established processes which enable it to understand the feelings, needs and motivations of its stakeholders. It uses this information to underpin its strategies, actions and decisions. Processes are established to manage relationships with all stakeholder groups.

Influence
Structures are in place to ensure that in interactions with all stakeholder groups the organisation is able to present persuasive arguments which will support the achievement of goals deemed to be aligned with the vision, values and business strategy.

Intuitiveness
Processes which are in place to encourage individuals and teams to make decisions, which are perceived as essential to business performance when faced with incomplete or ambiguous information. The extent to which the organisation values and supports the use of individual experience and intuition, based on this experience, in the decision-making process.

Conscientiousness
What the organisation says in public, its advertising, PR and espoused values are consistent with how people experience the organisation. In addition, the organisation's behaviour is perceived to be in line with the prevailing ethical behaviour that society expects.

Malcolm Higgs and Mary McGuire used this instrument in a study involving nine organisations and 164 participants. Multiple ratings of culture using the EICA were compared with average levels of individual emotional intelligence (measured using the EIQ: M). Statistically significant relationships were found between all elements of emotional intelligence and the cultural dimensions. Furthermore, the study showed that the EICA was a reliable instrument. In addition, the study provided some evidence to the assertions we made above in terms of the relationship between EI and culture in relation to the Goffee and Jones culture model.

Using this framework, is it possible to position organisations (using publicly available data) in terms of their organisational emotional intelligence? We believe that it is and have decided to use our knowledge (which is based on publicly available data) to present some illustrations of organisations which may be seen at the extremes on each of the scales of emotional intelligence. Business changes rapidly and there is always a danger of being overtaken by such changes when writing about organisations. The examples we have selected are based on the organisations in the context of the late 1990s. The summary of our initial viewpoint is shown in **Table 10.3**. While we accept that this is far from complete or robust it does, we believe, demonstrate the complexity of emotional intelligence and the challenges of building an emotionally intelligent organisation. While our examples demonstrate a range of 'high and lows' on the organisational profile in relation to the components of emotional intelligence (for example we would see Body Shop as high on self-awareness, motivation, influence and conscientiousness) we can see the same organisations as low on other components (emotional resilience and intuitiveness). At this point we would declare that this (without further evidence) is unfair to a single organisation (e.g. our illustration of Body Shop). However, we believe it illustrates the principle in a way in which we can experience and understand organisations as an outsider. Similarly those which appear, as organisations with high emotional intelligence seem to score well across all scales and thus demonstrate **balance** (for example Virgin and Hewlett Packard).

The 'evidence' on which we base our attribution is that which is in the public arena and is summarised very briefly below. However, we are aware of how rapidly the interpretation of public data can be turned on its head. For example, the collapse of Enron in 2002 has totally repositioned our thinking about a number of businesses. In reading these examples, please reflect on the context of the perceptions of the organisation at that time.

Table 10.3: Organisations and Emotional Intelligence

EI Factor	High EI	Low EI
Self-awareness	• Body Shop • Virgin • Hewlett Packard	• Microsoft • UK financial services
Emotional Resilience	• Virgin • Benetton	• Shell • Body Shop
Motivation	• Ford • Hewlett Packard • Wrigleys	• European financial sector
Interpersonal Sensitivity	• Virgin • Hewlett Packard	• Microsoft • Marks & Spencer • Benetton
Intuitiveness	• Virgin • Monsanto	• European financial sector
Influence	• British Airways • Virgin • Body Shop	• Monsanto
Conscientiousness	• Ben & Jerry's • Virgin	• Maxwell Communications • Polly Peck

Self-awareness

Both the ethical trading policies and focus on ethical development of pharmaceuticals have figured highly in the development of Body Shop. Many of their actions, advertising campaigns and public statements have tended to highlight their acute awareness of how they **feel** about the reactions of others to their decisions and to disclose the underlying importance of their feelings about their business. Similar comments may be made about the UK organisation Virgin and the high tech company Hewlett Packard. These organisations all appear to show a clear vision which has an emotional as well as business intent.

At the other extreme, the descriptions we read about the legal challenges in the US facing Microsoft indicate a relatively low level of organisational self-awareness. Similarly in the UK many financial services organisations faced with regulatory mis-selling actions appear to demonstrate low levels of organisational self-awareness.

Emotional Resilience

While Body Shop could be seen as an organisation with high self-awareness (prior to recent changes in ownership) the way in which it was affected by a challenge to its image (as reported in the media) could indicate relatively low emotional resilience. Contrast this with the way in which Benetton responded to attacks on its somewhat controversial advertising campaigns which illustrate relatively high levels of resilience. Shell, when facing attack in relation to a number of environmental issues has appeared to exhibit low levels of emotional resilience, while Virgin, having ventured into the UK railways market and being sharply criticised appears to exhibit high levels of resilience.

Motivation

In the context of emotional intelligence, motivation is about 'long-termism' and persistence. Organisations such as Ford, Hewlett Packard, Virgin and Wrigleys have all provided illustrations of sticking to decisions which underpin long-term strategies and forge short-term opportunities for financial gains or savings. A classic example of this is the fact that Wrigleys continued to advertise their product in the UK during World War II despite the fact that the product was not available, and would not be available, until the conclusion of the war. On the other hand organisations with relatively low levels of motivation (in emotional intelligence terms) will take the short-term gains at the potential expense of failing to achieve long-term goals or financial returns. It is difficult to provide specific organisational examples, but it is possible to see that many players in the financial sector fall into this category.

Interpersonal Sensitivity

Organisations which appear to place a premium on understanding the feelings, needs and motivations of stakeholders include Virgin and Hewlett Packard. At the other end of the scale we once again return to the legal challenges to Microsoft which appear to be exacerbated by inattention to the interests of stakeholders; the decline in performance of Marks & Spencer, the retail chain, which appeared (until late 2001) to have failed to be sensitive to the management of all stakeholder needs; and the impact on Benetton of the failure to consider the needs and feelings of its stakeholders.

Intuitiveness

The link between the needs of stakeholders being balanced with the long-term aspirations of the business in the light of incomplete or ambiguous information characterise this element of organisational emotional intelligence. Once again Virgin provide an example of a high EI organisation in this factor. Their entry into the UK financial sector market in the early 1990s against a background of increasing regulation, competition and uncertainty with no clear parameters for determining success represents a clear example of EI intuitiveness. Similarly Monsanto's decision to invest heavily in the area of genetically modified crops in the midst of scientific, political and social ambiguity provides another clear example of organisational intuitiveness in EI terms.

The extent to which mergers of many organisations in the European financial sector have been hinted at, explored and ultimately abandoned illustrate a potential lack of intuitiveness in EI terms.

Influence

Virgin provide a clear example of the organisational ability to influence stakeholders involving brand image and investor support. Similarly British Airways, in spite of long-term domestic and performance problems, has been able to demonstrate such levels of influence. In spite of media reports and attacks of interest groups Body Shop has demonstrated abilities which match our description of EI influence. However, in the debate over genetically modified crops Monsanto appear to have relatively low levels of Influence.

Conscientiousness

This is, perhaps, the most difficult area in which to provide examples (particularly negative ones). Within the UK, high profile examples of low levels of conscientiousness would be provided by organisations such as Polly Peck and Maxwell Communications which were surrounded by unethical (and indeed illegal) practices. Similar issues have arisen in the US with Enron and Worldcom. Organisations demonstrating high levels of conscientiousness include Virgin (who have demonstrated this in a public and high profile way) and the US-based ice cream chain, Ben & Jerry's who contributed a percentage of all sales to charitable causes, a value which pervaded the organisation.

From the comments above it is evident that the concept of emotional intelligence has potential meaning and benefits for both individuals and organisations.

Implications

As an individual, the need to consider how the organisation in which we do, or may, work will support or punish emotional intelligence can be an important consideration in our own career planning. Based on an understanding of our own emotional intelligence, if we can identify the emotional intelligence of the company we work for, or intend to work for, then we can identify a potential career strategy. Such choices are illustrated in **Figure 10.6**.

Figure 10.6: Emotional Intelligence: Personal/Organisational Fit

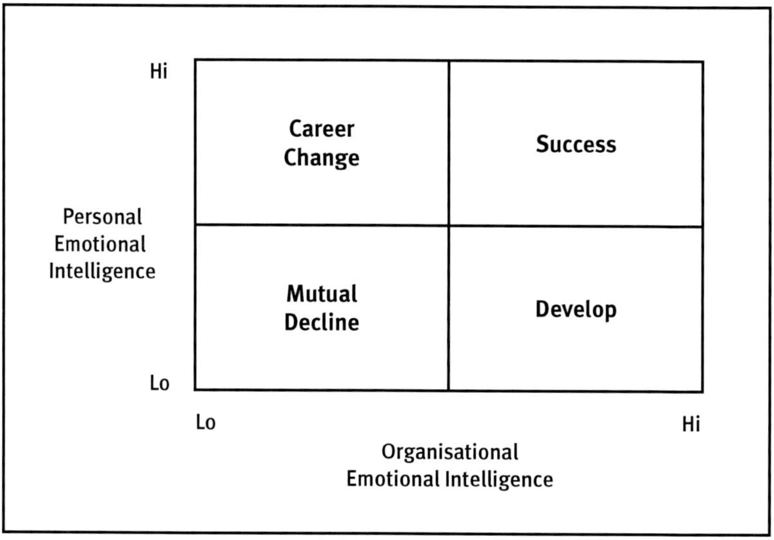

If an individual has a high emotional intelligence and works in a low EI company he/she should look elsewhere for career development. Alternatively, if an individual is in a 'high EI' company, but has low personal EI then an attempt should be made to develop emotional intelligence as this would be both supported and beneficial.

How Emotionally Intelligent is My Organisation?

In order to match ourselves to our organisation, we need a view on the EI of our organisation. While there is no established 'test' to measure the EI of organisations, a somewhat simplistic list of questions can prove to be a relatively useful guide. Such a list is as shown in **Table 10.4**.

Table 10.4: Checking Organisational and Emotional Intelligence

	High	Medium	Low
• Does the organisation have a clear vision?			
• Are there regular customer surveys?			
• Are there regular employee satisfaction surveys?			
• If the organisation is 'attacked' by the media are responses quick and credible?			
• Do external 'attacks' deflect the organisation from its long-term plans?			
• Are decisions based on long-term goals or short-term/opportunistic profits?			
• Is a lot of effort put into internal communications?			
• If morale changes, does the organisation react quickly and appropriately?			
• Do all people have a clear view of the organisation's long-term goals?			
• Are all actions consistent with the organisation's stated vision, values and goals?			
• Are values clear?			
• Do you know how you are expected to behave?			
• Does the organisation invest effort in trying to understand the needs of all stakeholders?			
• Are you clear about who the stakeholders are?			
• Are decision-making processes clear and consistent?			
• Is there congruence between the stated position and values of the organisation and how it conducts its business?			

The list in **Table 10.4** is by no means a comprehensive or 'scientific' basis for evaluating the emotional intelligence of an organisation. However, the more questions you answer positively from this list, the more likely you are to be in an organisation with high emotional intelligence. This, in turn, helps you to make important personal and career development decisions.

Some Concluding Thoughts

Throughout this book, and indeed in our work to date, we have focused on emotional intelligence in a work context. Our frame of reference, thus far, has been the growth in interest in the topic in the broader context of organisations seeing 'people as a competitive advantage' and attempting to translate this into practical realities. This journey has, inevitably, caused us to reflect on the question: 'What does all this mean for the individual?' While we have addressed this, in part, our response has again been set in a work context. Even in this clearly delineated context the exploration of emotional intelligence has raised questions. Our work to date has focused on using the assessment of emotional intelligence as a basis for development. The key questions we have been faced with are (in the organisational context):

- Can we use this as a basis for selection?
- Is it helpful in **predicting** potential for senior management, for CEOs, etc.?
- Will it help us to pick the right graduates to join us?

However, in working with individuals we have been asked interestingly different questions, including:

- How does this relate to my career?
- Does it have applications outside work?
- Is this an aid to counselling?
- Can it help individuals experiencing stress or other work-related issues?

Furthermore, given the media's interest in the topic, we have been asked questions relating to the implications of emotional intelligence for educational principles and practices. Perhaps the only question we have not been asked to date is: 'How does emotional intelligence explain the meaning of life?'

We do not intend to be flippant at this stage in the book. However, we do feel that it is important to draw a clear line between what we believe is known and what, as yet, belongs in the realm which could be labelled 'still to be explored'. In this chapter we have attempted to address these issues and link them to the commonly raised questions.

Careers

The core proposition which we have explored in relation to emotional intelligence and careers in this book relates to the research that demonstrates that it is EQ (given an acceptable level of IQ) which distinguishes between success and average progression in an individual's chosen career or profession. However, as we pointed out in **chapter 10**, some organisations are fertile ground for individuals with high emotional intelligence, while others are not. Individuals need to reflect on the match between their emotional intelligence and their perceptions of the EI Friendly or Supporting/EI Punishing characteristics of the organisation they are either working within or seeking to join.

What we do not, as yet, know is what types of career are best suited to individuals who have high levels of emotional intelligence, and which should be avoided. However, some of our research has shown some interesting links to specific roles and associated profiles of those roles in EI terms (e.g. the studies referred to in **chapter 3**). However, further research is clearly needed to explore the role which emotional intelligence can play in career guidance and discussion.

Relationships

We are very clear that our work to date, and this book, have focused on emotional intelligence in a business or work context. However, we are equally aware that emotional intelligence has clear antecedents and linkages to the arena of individual counselling. Hopefully the reader will be able to draw lessons from the work context which they can bring to bear in managing personal relationships in a broader 'life' context. We are reluctant to go beyond such a broad statement in this book. As yet the research into this topic from a business perspective has not been integrated into developments and practices in the field of broader 'life' counselling and development. It is our genuine hope that our work may contribute to such an holistic perspective.

Personal Issues/Challenges

In part this area is explored in our comments in the above section. If, for example, we were to be asked to look at the relationship between emotional intelligence and stress at work we would propose that two issues need to be explored:

(a) The relationship between the individual's emotional intelligence profile and the organisational culture. Clearly, individuals who are high on most elements of emotional intelligence and who work in an organisation which does not encourage, support or value such behaviours will undergo a degree of personal stress. A contributory factor in managing such stress will be the ability of the individual to understand (in EI terms) its causes and develop appropriate adaptive strategies.

(b) The understanding of the individual's level of emotional resilience (one of the EI factors). Individuals with relatively low levels of emotional resilience should seek to develop this element as one of their strategies for stress management.

However, more recent research which we have been involved with does demonstrate that high EI is associated clearly with lower levels of stress.

Education

Much of the early literature on emotional intelligence has drawn from research in the field of education and development. However, this literature (and the associated research) focuses on the children/students rather than on the teachers. We would contend, from our research and experience, that much can be learned from studies of the emotional intelligence of the teachers, and the relative success of differing levels of this in terms of pupil/student behaviours and successes. In many ways what we have learned in respect of the importance of emotional intelligence for managers applies directly to teachers (in the educational context) and contains significant transferable learning.

Selection of People

Our framework for examining emotional intelligence has been essentially developmental. In essence, our questions have been 'How can you measure and develop an individual's emotional intelligence in a business or organisational context?' The extension of this line of enquiry to personnel selection applications needs to be approached carefully. For example, before pursuing such a route any organisation would need to be sure that selecting 'high EQ' individuals would contribute to the achievement of their strategic goals to be culturally sustainable.

The research and data, available to date, examines differences in 'success' and 'performance' among individuals already in-post. Further research would be necessary in order to establish the predictive validity (among new entrant populations) of emotional intelligence measures. We do know that a number of organisations have begun this work and are now using EI as a part of a structured selection process.

At present, the understanding of emotional intelligence (and its associated measurement) could contribute to a selection decision as part of a broad and robust process. For example, an assessment of emotional intelligence could have a place in an assessment centre, used for selection purposes, as one source of input (along with others). In this way the EI data could be used by assessors as a further source which could assist them in refining judgements against a number of target criteria. For internal assessment centres, the use of the 360° questionnaire will enhance the contribution of EI to such selection decisions.

Assessment of Potential

Given the points which we made in **chapter 8** it is inevitable that the question arises 'does emotional intelligence predict leadership potential?' To a large extent our answer to this question mirrors our answer to the question on emotional intelligence and selection. In many ways the identification of leadership potential represents an 'advanced selection' consideration. In our view, given the research evidence to date, the level of an individual's emotional intelligence, in organisations which place value on these characteristics, can be a helpful input to a process for identifying an individual's potential. Furthermore, it can be helpful to use the assessment of an individual's emotional intelligence to formulate a development plan which, in the right organisational context, will assist them in realising their leadership potential (assessed against a broader range of criteria). Overall we are conscious of the tendency of organisations to seek a simplistic or 'black box' means of ensuring that they pick the 'right' future leaders. However, such decisions are complex and capable of being informed by relatively sophisticated (albeit resource intensive) methods of assessment. The 'bad news' for organisations requiring a 'quick fix' solution to the potential identification issue is that emotional intelligence does not provide it. While we have found some evidence of links between EI and leadership potential (see **chapter 8**) it is clear that further research is required to establish a definite relationship between an individual's emotional intelligence and their leadership potential. However, reviewing **chapter 8** it is evident that such research is likely to be fruitful.

Conclusions

Although much work on the examination of EI has taken place since this book was first published, we are aware that the topic remains potentially controversial. While much of the new research data provided by ourselves and others reaffirms the significance of EI and its robustness as a concept, it has also served to raise further questions. What is now even clearer is that the concept of emotional intelligence is well grounded. It is more than re-packaging of old ideas or a branch of 'new age' thinking. It has real implications for businesses and those who work within them. Furthermore, its emergence as an idea is timely in terms of the emergence of new models relating to businesses and their strategies (particularly in a global context). As with many new ideas in the business world, there is a tendency to overstate the case. What is known and proved about emotional intelligence represents an extension of decades of work designed to inform our understanding of the relationship between individual characteristics, success and work. What is often claimed exceeds what is known and can be proven.

In many ways, emotional intelligence, as a concept, is of value to both individuals and organisations (as has been discussed in the previous chapters). This may be a timely concept in the context of the 'new employment deal' or 'new psychological contract'. In this book we have not set out to 'make the case for emotional intelligence', but to 'make sense of emotional intelligence'. Others have 'made the case'; hopefully we have contributed to the discussion. In terms of 'making sense' we hope that we have helped the reader to understand the nature of emotional intelligence and its place in a broader organisational context. Furthermore, we hope that we have hinted at (if not nailed down) the case for individuals to reflect on their own emotional intelligence.

In the realms of personality we are always forced to take a position on the classic 'nature/nurture' argument. In the case of emotional intelligence, are you born with it or can you develop it? Our response, we are very aware, runs the risk of a classic consultant response which is positioned contextually with the phrase 'Well it depends ...'. When pushed, we believe that a significant element of emotional intelligence is capable of development.

Finally, we do hope that we have presented an exciting picture of the nature and potential of emotional intelligence and highlighted some interesting and challenging areas for future study which will ensure that the topic does not suffer the consequences of a 'flavour of the month' business issue. We believe that the journey to understand and apply emotional intelligence is far from complete. Indeed, while the past few years has built our understanding of the concept, we believe that there is much more to be explored, and, furthermore, this offers an exciting prospect. We truly hope that, having read this book, you share our view and our excitement.

APPENDICES: SAMPLE REPORTS

I. Emotional Intelligence Questionnaire:
   Managerial

II. Emotional Intelligence Questionnaire:
    Managerial 360°

APPENDIX I

EMOTIONAL INTELLIGENCE QUESTIONNAIRE:

MANAGERIAL

Report on:
Ms Sample
30 October 2002

Supplied by PreVisor.
Published by PreVisor Inc., Arlington Square, Downshire Way, Bracknell, Berkshire, RG12 1WA, UK.

IMPORTANT NOTE
This report was produced by software which is available only to individuals who have undertaken approved training in the use of the Emotional Intelligence Questionnaire: Managerial. The descriptions of emotional intelligence it contains are not absolute truths, but are based upon the research and experience of the Authors. It is possible that the person described in the report may disagree with parts of it despite the Authors' efforts to ensure that the statements contained in the report are an accurate reflection of the person's responses to the questionnaire. Because of this, it is recommended that the report be presented to both the respondent and third parties (such as recruiters, trainers and counsellors) on a person-to-person basis. Whenever this report is used to make decisions concerning the respondent, all other available information of relevance, such as his/her track record and ability, should be taken into account.

EMOTIONAL INTELLIGENCE QUESTIONNAIRE: MANAGERIAL

REPORT

INTRODUCTION

This report provides information, based on your response to the Emotional Intelligence Questionnaire: Managerial. It reviews your results on the seven elements which comprise the overall emotional intelligence (EI) result. In recent research studies, a high level of emotional intelligence has been found to be associated with 'success' in a work context. Indeed, some claim that high emotional intelligence is associated with more wide-reaching 'life success'.

However, in interpreting your results, it is important to understand how the different elements of your emotional intelligence contribute to the overall result. All results are examined in relation to a reference group, comparing your responses to the distribution of results from a large sample of managers, to determine objectively your emotional intelligence profile and its implications. It is useful to examine the individual element results in order to identify which components of emotional intelligence you might wish to reinforce, or develop, to enhance your performance. Your overall EI result is also reported.

In reviewing your results, it is helpful to begin by reading the definition of the element being reported. You will find this reproduced just below the title of each element. Any results below the average range will give you some indication of development priorities, while any above-average results will reflect a strength you may wish to apply more widely.

The seven elements of emotional intelligence

A   Self-awareness

The awareness of one's own feelings and the capability to recognise and manage these feelings in a way which one feels that one can control. This factor includes a degree of self-belief in one's capability to manage one's emotions and to control their impact in a work environment.

Your self-assessment for this element is higher than that of most of the comparison group. This indicates that you are likely to be highly aware of your own feelings in a range of work-related situations, and can remain in control of your emotions and feelings. You may find it helpful to reflect on your capabilities to manage your feelings in diverse situations and become even more conscious of the way in which this is translated into practical behaviours. This process of thinking about and reinforcing your awareness may help to ensure that you apply the behaviours in a productive and consistent manner.

B   Emotional resilience

The capability to perform consistently in a range of situations under pressure and to adapt behaviour appropriately. The capability to balance the needs of the situation and task with the needs and concerns of the individuals involved. The capability to retain focus on a course of action or need for results in the face of personal challenge or criticism.

On this scale your self-assessment indicates that you are in the lower range for the element. Such a score could indicate that you find it difficult to perform consistently when under pressure. It might indicate that you can become frustrated by challenge or criticism and therefore find it difficult to continue to perform effectively in these circumstances. A helpful way of developing this element is to attempt to depersonalise criticism and challenge, and view it as a challenge to the ideas, proposals, etc. associated with the task rather than a personal attack. It can be useful to engage others in discussion to review the problem and task from different perspectives in order to find a successful way forward.

C Motivation

The drive and energy to achieve clear results and make an impact and, also, to balance short- and long-term goals with a capability to pursue demanding goals in the face of rejection or questioning.

Your self-assessment on this element produces a result which is in the lower range. Such a score could indicate that you have a tendency to focus on short-term goals and actions at the expense of clear long-term goals or aspirations. Indeed, it might be a result of your having no strong long-term goal to which you feel sufficiently committed and which you believe worth pursuing, even in the face of opposition. In order to develop this element you might find it helpful to reflect on your aspirations in a work context and identify the longer-term goals which you believe to be essential for realising these aspirations. You may then find it easier to achieve a balance between short-term goals and actions and the longer-term goal.

D Interpersonal sensitivity

The capability to be aware of, and take account of, the needs and perceptions of others in arriving at decisions and proposing solutions to problems and challenges. The capability to build from this awareness and achieve the commitment of others to decisions and action ideas. The willingness to keep open one's thoughts on possible solutions to problems and to actively listen to, and reflect on, the reactions and inputs from others.

On this scale your self-assessment indicates that you are highly sensitive to other people. Therefore, you are likely to engage others in problem-solving and decision-making. In dealing with others you are likely to listen carefully and acknowledge their uncertainties, needs, views and opinions. It may be useful for you to identify the behaviours which lead to this understanding and the capability to engage and involve others, and ensure that you apply them consistently in all work situations.

E Influence

The capability to persuade others to change a viewpoint based on the understanding of their position and the recognition of the need to listen to this perspective and provide a rationale for change.

On this scale your self-assessment indicates that you are in the average range. Such a score on this element could indicate that you may find that, in some situations, it is not always easy for you to win others over to your point of view. You may sometimes feel frustrated by your inability to persuade others to change their viewpoint or opinion on an important issue. A helpful way of developing capability in this area is to reflect on those situations in which you have been successful in influencing others. In doing this, try to identify the behaviours or strategies which worked and then try to apply them to all situations in which you need to influence others.

In reflecting on your development of influence, you might consider the following strengths indicated by your self-assessment: establishing rapport with external contacts. A development plan which builds on these strengths may be an effective way of enhancing your capability in influence.

F Intuitiveness

The capability to arrive at clear decisions and drive their implementation when presented with incomplete or ambiguous information using both rational and 'emotional' or intuitive perceptions of key issues and implications.

Your self-assessment on this element produces a result which is in the lower range. Such a score could indicate that you are uncomfortable making decisions unless you have full and unambiguous data available. It may be that you either lack the confidence to use your own experience to close any gaps in information, or believe such intuitive behaviour would lead to an incorrect or bad decision. One useful way of developing capabilities in this area is to reflect on past business decisions you have made. In doing so, try to identify the decision you would have made before you had all the information you felt to be necessary. Then compare this to the final decision. You may find, from this, that your own experience led to intuitive decisions which were close to the final ones. Try applying the insight from these reflections to your future decisions.

G   Conscientiousness

The capability to display clear commitment to a course of action in the face of challenge and to match 'words and deeds' in encouraging others to support the chosen direction. The personal commitment to pursuing an ethical solution to a difficult business issue or problem.

On this scale your self-assessment shows a high level of conscientiousness. This indicates that your words and actions are likely to be consistent. It is also likely that you demonstrate a high degree of personal commitment to both goals and behaviours. In general, you are likely to achieve high levels of performance without resorting to pragmatic behaviour and are likely to demonstrate high ethical standards. It may be helpful for you to recognise the impact of such behaviours on others and ensure that you apply them to a wide range of challenges and situations.

Overall emotional intelligence

Your overall result, based on your self-assessment, indicates that you are in the average range. In order to identify how you might begin to develop your effectiveness in a work context, review the profile of your scores on the seven elements. If almost all scores fall within the average range (around five or six) then some limited action across a broad range of elements would seem to be called for. However, it is important, in maintaining commitment to development, to secure some 'quick wins'. Therefore, your priorities for action could well be in relation to those elements where clear strengths are indicated which you would build on to secure a relatively rapid improvement in your performance. If, however, your average overall score results from a mixture of high and low element scores it makes sense to focus your efforts on development actions designed to address improvements on the low-scoring elements.

DEVELOPMENT GUIDELINES

It is possible to develop your overall level of emotional intelligence by planned and sustained development activities. If you wish to develop your capabilities in this area, a useful framework is as follows:

- reflect on, and identify, examples of behaviour which you exhibit in different situations;

- identify those behaviours which are seen as strengths in this report, and develop plans to strengthen and build on these;

- identify those behaviours which are seen as development needs in this report, and identify changes which you could make to address these needs;

- consciously practise reinforcing and changing behaviours, and reflect on your responses to them;

- continuously seek feedback from colleagues on the behaviour you have attempted to change.

The overall development guidelines in your self-report are important. However, with the benefit of feedback from others you can reflect on how they have perceived your reactions to significant events, challenges or decisions. You could also benefit from discussing your development actions and ideas with colleagues. This will enable you to fine tune your proposed action plans.

Emotional Intelligence Questionnaire: Managerial

Self-Assessment Profile Chart

Name: Ms Sample

Sten	1	2	3	4	5	6	7	8	9	10	
A	.	.	.	.	.	.	7	.	.	.	Self-awareness
B	.	.	.	4	.	.	.	.	.	.	Emotional resilience
C	.	2	.	.	.	.	.	.	.	.	Motivation
D	.	.	.	.	.	.	.	8	.	.	Interpersonal sensitivity
E	.	.	.	.	5	.	.	.	.	.	Influence
F	.	2	.	.	.	.	.	.	.	.	Intuitiveness
G	.	.	.	.	.	.	.	8	.	.	Conscientiousness
EI	.	.	.	.	5	.	.	.	.	.	Overall EI
Percentile	1	4	11	23	40	60	77	89	96	99	

Norms used: All Managers

APPENDIX II

EMOTIONAL INTELLIGENCE QUESTIONNAIRE:

MANAGERIAL 360°

**Report on:
Mr Sample
30 October 2002**

Supplied by PreVisor.
Published by PreVisor Inc., Arlington Square, Downshire Way,
Bracknell, Berkshire, RG12 1WA, UK.

EMOTIONAL INTELLIGENCE QUESTIONNAIRE: MANAGERIAL 360°

REPORT

REPORT FORMAT

This report is based on your completion of the Emotional Intelligence Questionnaire: Managerial, and the 360° version of the questionnaire completed by one or more colleagues who were able to comment on your behaviours in a work-related context. 'Colleagues' can include your boss, peers and subordinates. The structure of this report is as follows.

Section 1: Results and interpretation

This section describes your emotional intelligence based upon the Emotional Intelligence Questionnaire: Managerial which you completed, together with the 360° questionnaires provided by your colleagues. It highlights any differences of opinion and possible areas on which to focus your development. In analysing the data provided, all scores have been normed against self-assessments from a managerial population.

Section 2: Analysis of colleagues' perceptions

This section examines how you can interpret differences between your own perceptions and those of your colleagues.

Section 3: Feedback from others and development

This section provides some very broad developmental guidelines and encourages you to discuss, in a non-judgemental way, the perceptions of your colleagues with them before finalising your development plan.

IMPORTANT NOTE

This report was produced by software which is available only to individuals who have undertaken approved training in the use of the Emotional Intelligence Questionnaire: Managerial. The descriptions of emotional intelligence it contains are not absolute truths, but are based upon the research and experience of the Authors. It is possible that the person described in the report may disagree with parts of it despite the Authors' efforts to ensure that the statements contained in the report are an accurate reflection of the person's responses to the questionnaire. Because of this, it is recommended that the report be presented to both the respondent and third parties (such as recruiters, trainers and counsellors) on a person-to-person basis. Whenever this report is used to make decisions concerning the respondent, all other available information of relevance, such as his/her track record and ability, should be taken into account.

SECTION 1: RESULTS AND INTERPRETATION

Introduction

This report provides information, based on your own response to the Emotional Intelligence Questionnaire: Managerial, and your colleagues' responses to the Emotional Intelligence Questionnaire: Managerial 360°. It reviews your results on the seven elements which comprise the overall emotional intelligence (EI) result. In recent research studies, a high level of emotional intelligence has been found to be associated with 'success' in a work context. Indeed, some claim that high emotional intelligence is associated with more wide-reaching 'life success'.

However, in interpreting your results, it is important to understand how the different elements of your emotional intelligence contribute to the overall result. All results are examined in relation to a reference group, comparing your and your colleagues' responses to the distribution of results from a large sample of managers, to determine objectively your emotional intelligence profile and its implications. It is useful to examine the individual element results in order to identify which components of emotional intelligence you might wish to reinforce, or develop, to enhance your performance. Your overall EI result is also examined at the end of this section.

In reviewing your results, it is helpful to begin by reading the definition of the element being reported. You will find this reproduced just below the title of each element. Any results below the average range will give you some indication of development priorities, while any above-average results will reflect a strength you may wish to apply more widely.

The seven elements of emotional intelligence

A   Self-awareness

The awareness of one's own feelings and the capability to recognise and manage these feelings in a way which one feels that one can control. This factor includes a degree of self-belief in one's capability to manage one's emotions and to control their impact in a work environment.

Your self-assessment for this element produces a result which is fairly typical of the comparison group's results. This could indicate that, while generally aware of your feelings and emotions in work situations, there are some situations in which this is not so. In order to develop this element further, you might find it helpful to reflect on specific situations in which you have felt in control of your feelings and emotions. In thinking about these situations you may be able to identify specific actions which were helpful. You could then apply these in a broader situation which arouses strong feelings or emotions. Those colleagues who completed the 360° questionnaire share your view as to your level of self-awareness. This consistency in perception is helpful in directing your development planning. You may, however, gain even greater insight by talking to your colleagues about their perceptions of your behaviour in a range of situations.

In reflecting on your development of self-awareness, you might consider the following strengths indicated by your self-assessment: functioning effectively when experiencing changing moods; understanding the reasons why you feel overwhelmed; and understanding the reasons for your emotional reactions, and then dealing with them. A development plan which builds on these strengths may be an effective way of enhancing your capability in self-awareness.

B Emotional resilience

The capability to perform consistently in a range of situations under pressure and to adapt behaviour appropriately. The capability to balance the needs of the situation and task with the needs and concerns of the individuals involved. The capability to retain focus on a course of action or need for results in the face of personal challenge or criticism.

On this scale your self-assessment indicates that you are in the lower range for the element. Such a score could indicate that you find it difficult to perform consistently when under pressure. A helpful way of developing this element is to attempt to depersonalise criticism and challenge, and view it as a challenge to the ideas, proposals, etc. associated with the task rather than a personal attack. It can be useful to engage others in discussion to review the problem and task from different perspectives in order to find a successful way forward. However, those colleagues who completed the 360° questionnaire see you as being somewhat more emotionally resilient than is suggested by your self-assessment. You could reflect on the possible reasons for this difference; for instance you may have been somewhat harsh with yourself in assessing this aspect of your emotional intelligence. It is important to gain some understanding of the factors that have led to this difference in perception before finalising the development ideas suggested by your self-assessment.

Developing your emotional resilience may be helped by building on your areas of particular strength which, according to your ratings were: adjusting to new situations and circumstances; and adapting your behaviour to different situations.

C Motivation

The drive and energy to achieve clear results and make an impact and, also, to balance short- and long-term goals with a capability to pursue demanding goals in the face of rejection or questioning.

Your self-assessment on this element produces a result which is in the lower range. Such a score could indicate that you have a tendency to focus on short-term goals and actions at the expense of clear long-term goals or aspirations. Indeed, it might be a result of your having no strong long-term goal to which you feel sufficiently committed and which you believe worth pursuing, even in the face of opposition. In order to develop this element you might find it helpful to reflect on your aspirations in a work context and identify the longer-term goals which you believe to be essential for realising these aspirations. You may then find it easier to achieve a balance between short-term goals and actions and the longer-term goal. However, those colleagues who completed the 360° questionnaire see you as being somewhat more motivated than is suggested by your self-assessment. You could reflect on the possible reasons for this difference; for instance you may have been somewhat harsh with yourself in assessing this aspect of your emotional intelligence. It is important to gain some understanding of the factors that have led to this difference in perception before finalising the development ideas suggested by your self-assessment.

Developing your motivation may be helped by building on your area of particular strength which, according to your ratings was: contributing to projects and tasks.

D   Interpersonal sensitivity

The capability to be aware of, and take account of, the needs and perceptions of others in arriving at decisions and proposing solutions to problems and challenges. The capability to build from this awareness and achieve the commitment of others to decisions and action ideas. The willingness to keep open one's thoughts on possible solutions to problems and to actively listen to, and reflect on, the reactions and inputs from others.

Your score on this element, based on your self-assessment, is in the average range. This could indicate that, while you sometimes take account of the views and feelings of others, there are situations in which you have a tendency to impose your own solutions on those you work with. In order to develop this element you might find it helpful to reflect on the situations in which you feel you have been successful and identify the behaviours you adopted. You could then try to apply these behaviours more generally in working with others. Those colleagues who completed the 360° questionnaire share your view as to your level of interpersonal sensitivity. This consistency in perception is helpful in directing your development planning. You may, however, gain even greater insight by talking to your colleagues about their perceptions of your behaviour in a range of situations.

In reflecting on your development of interpersonal sensitivity, you might consider the following strengths indicated by your self-assessment: taking account of contributions from others; and taking greater account of the views of others when making decisions. A development plan which builds on these strengths may be an effective way of enhancing your capability in interpersonal sensitivity.

E   Influence

The capability to persuade others to change a viewpoint based on the understanding of their position and the recognition of the need to listen to this perspective and provide a rationale for change.

On this scale your self-assessment indicates that you are in the average range. Such a score on this element could indicate that you may find that, in some situations, it is not always easy for you to win others over to your point of view. You may sometimes feel frustrated by your inability to persuade others to change their viewpoint or opinion on an important issue. A helpful way of developing capability in this area is to reflect on those situations in which you have been successful in influencing others. In doing this, try to identify the behaviours or strategies which worked and then try to apply them to all situations in which you need to influence others. Compared with your self-assessment, others see you as being significantly more influential than you do yourself. You may find it helpful to reflect on specific incidents and to focus on possible explanations for this difference in perception. If possible, explore with your colleagues the reasons for their ratings of your behaviour. The outcomes of these discussions can help when planning your development.

In reflecting on your development of influence, you might consider the following strengths indicated by your self-assessment: persuading others to listen to, and take account of your comments. A development plan which builds on these strengths may be an effective way of enhancing your capability in influence.

F   Intuitiveness

The capability to arrive at clear decisions and drive their implementation when presented with incomplete or ambiguous information using both rational and 'emotional' or intuitive perceptions of key issues and implications.

On this scale your self-assessment shows a high score. This indicates that you are able to make decisions in difficult situations when faced with incomplete or ambiguous information. In such situations it is likely that you will use your previous experience as a basis for an intuitive assessment of the decision. It may be helpful for you to reflect on and understand the way in which you make these decisions and the way you communicate them to others. Using this understanding could help ensure that you make consistent and appropriate use of this capability. Those colleagues who completed the 360° questionnaire share your view as to your level of intuitiveness. This consistency in perception is helpful in directing your development planning. You may, however, gain even greater insight by talking to your colleagues about their perceptions of your behaviour in a range of situations.

G   Conscientiousness

The capability to display clear commitment to a course of action in the face of challenge and to match 'words and deeds' in encouraging others to support the chosen direction. The personal commitment to pursuing an ethical solution to a difficult business issue or problem.

On this scale your self-assessment indicates that you are in the lower range for the element. Such a score on this scale indicates that you may, on occasions, choose to be unduly pragmatic and probably be willing to 'bend the rules' to get a task completed or achieve a particular goal. The self-assessment on this scale indicates that you may find that others perceive inconsistency between your words and your actions in practice. Developing your capability on this element may be helped by finding ways of achieving results within the organisation's existing standards of behaviour. Developing consistency in behaviour may be helped by

Emotional Intelligence Questionnaire:
Managerial 360°

Self-Assessment Profile Chart

Name: Mr Sample

Sten	1	2	3	4	5	6	7	8	9	10	
A	.	.	.	.	.	6	.	.	.	.	Self-awareness
B	.	.	.	4	.	.	.	.	.	.	Emotional resilience
C	.	.	.	4	.	.	.	.	.	.	Motivation
D	.	.	.	.	.	6	.	.	.	.	Interpersonal sensitivity
E	.	.	.	.	5	.	.	.	.	.	Influence
F	.	.	.	.	.	.	.	.	9	.	Intuitiveness
G	.	2	.	.	.	.	.	.	.	.	Conscientiousness
EI	.	.	.	.	5	.	.	.	.	.	Overall EI
Percentile	1	4	11	23	40	60	77	89	96	99	

Norms used: International Management Sample

F   Intuitiveness

The capability to arrive at clear decisions and drive their implementation when presented with incomplete or ambiguous information using both rational and 'emotional' or intuitive perceptions of key issues and implications.

On this scale your self-assessment shows a high score. This indicates that you are able to make decisions in difficult situations when faced with incomplete or ambiguous information. In such situations it is likely that you will use your previous experience as a basis for an intuitive assessment of the decision. It may be helpful for you to reflect on and understand the way in which you make these decisions and the way you communicate them to others. Using this understanding could help ensure that you make consistent and appropriate use of this capability. Those colleagues who completed the 360° questionnaire share your view as to your level of intuitiveness. This consistency in perception is helpful in directing your development planning. You may, however, gain even greater insight by talking to your colleagues about their perceptions of your behaviour in a range of situations.

G   Conscientiousness

The capability to display clear commitment to a course of action in the face of challenge and to match 'words and deeds' in encouraging others to support the chosen direction. The personal commitment to pursuing an ethical solution to a difficult business issue or problem.

On this scale your self-assessment indicates that you are in the lower range for the element. Such a score on this scale indicates that you may, on occasions, choose to be unduly pragmatic and probably be willing to 'bend the rules' to get a task completed or achieve a particular goal. The self-assessment on this scale indicates that you may find that others perceive inconsistency between your words and your actions in practice. Developing your capability on this element may be helped by finding ways of achieving results within the organisation's existing standards of behaviour. Developing consistency in behaviour may be helped by

reflecting before acting, and testing whether or not your proposed action is in line with what you have said to others about a task, situation or problem. Compared with your self-assessment, others see you as being significantly more conscientious than you do yourself. You may find it helpful to reflect on specific incidents and to focus on possible explanations for this difference in perception. If possible, explore with your colleagues the reasons for their ratings of your behaviour. The outcomes of these discussions can help when planning your development.

Developing your conscientiousness may be helped by building on your areas of particular strength which, according to your ratings were: being dissatisfied with only average personal performance; and understanding the reasons for personal distress, and then dealing with it.

Overall emotional intelligence

Your overall result, based on your self-assessment, indicates that you are in the average range. In order to identify how you might begin to develop your effectiveness in a work context, review the profile of your scores on the seven elements. If almost all scores fall within the average range (around five or six) then some limited action across a broad range of elements would seem to be called for. However, it is important, in maintaining commitment to development, to secure some 'quick wins'. Therefore, your priorities for action could well be in relation to those elements where clear strengths are indicated which you would build on to secure a relatively rapid improvement in your performance. If, however, your average overall score results from a mixture of high and low element scores it makes sense to focus your efforts on development actions designed to address improvements on the low-scoring elements.

In examining the profile derived from your colleagues' assessment it appears that they have a somewhat more positive view of your overall level of emotional intelligence than you do. While at an overall level this

may indicate that you have been somewhat harsh on yourself it is important to look at the profile charts to ascertain whether your colleagues see the difference as being consistent across all elements or whether the overall result is influenced by significant differences in perception on a relatively few elements.

You will find a more detailed analysis of your colleagues' perceptions in section 2.

Emotional Intelligence Questionnaire: Managerial 360°

Self-Assessment Profile Chart

Name: Mr Sample

Sten	1	2	3	4	5	6	7	8	9	10	
A	.	.	.	.	.	6	.	.	.	.	Self-awareness
B	.	.	.	4	.	.	.	.	.	.	Emotional resilience
C	.	.	.	4	.	.	.	.	.	.	Motivation
D	.	.	.	.	.	6	.	.	.	.	Interpersonal sensitivity
E	.	.	.	.	5	.	.	.	.	.	Influence
F	.	.	.	.	.	.	.	.	9	.	Intuitiveness
G	.	2	.	.	.	.	.	.	.	.	Conscientiousness
EI	.	.	.	.	5	.	.	.	.	.	Overall EI
Percentile	1	4	11	23	40	60	77	89	96	99	

Norms used: International Management Sample

Emotional Intelligence Questionnaire: Managerial 360°

Colleagues' Profile Chart

Name: Mr Sample

Sten	1	2	3	4	5	6	7	8	9	10	
A	.	.	.	.	5	.	.	.	.	.	Self-awareness
B	.	.	.	.	.	6	.	.	.	.	Emotional resilience
C	.	.	.	.	.	.	7	.	.	.	Motivation
D	.	.	.	.	5	.	.	.	.	.	Interpersonal sensitivity
E	.	.	.	.	.	.	.	.	9	.	Influence
F	.	.	.	.	.	.	.	8	.	.	Intuitiveness
G	.	.	.	.	.	.	7	.	.	.	Conscientiousness
EI	.	.	.	.	.	.	7	.	.	.	Overall EI
Percentile	1	4	11	23	40	60	77	89	96	99	

Norms used: International Management Sample

SECTION 2: ANALYSIS OF COLLEAGUES' PERCEPTIONS

When reviewing the feedback from your colleagues it is important to focus on areas of agreement and disagreement. The feedback from colleagues has been analysed to provide an overall profile (shown on the preceding page), based on their most common responses to the questions. The differences between your own and your colleagues' assessments, and the implications of these differences, are highlighted and discussed in section 1.

While responding to the feedback it could be helpful for you to reflect on the similarities and differences between your self-assessment and the assessment provided by your colleagues. In reviewing these differences it is important to recognise that your own assessment may differ from that of your colleagues because of differences in perception. It could prove valuable for you to explore these differences by seeking the opportunity to learn and develop, rather than by becoming overly concerned with the correctness (in an absolute sense) of either assessment. For example, if you have a more positive overall view of your emotional intelligence, it may be more useful if you try to understand the reasons for the difference, rather than trying to identify which view is 'correct'.

In reviewing your colleagues' profile of you and comparing it with your own, it might be useful to consider the degree of difference between the two profiles. The table below shows the 'overall difference score', reflecting the difference between your own and your colleagues' profiles, based on the mode (most frequent) or, if there is not a mode, the mean (average) score.

'Difference score' between your profile and the average of your colleagues' profiles

Sten	1	2	3	4	5	6	7	8	9	10	
	.	.	.	.	.	.	.	8	.	.	Difference score
Percentile	1	4	11	23	40	60	77	89	96	99	

There is a relatively large difference between your own view of your emotional intelligence and the combined views of your colleagues.

A detailed analysis of where differences do occur shows that your colleagues see your emotional intelligence more positively than you do yourself. You might reflect on the possible reasons for this, and consider development actions and goals which are more stretching than they would have been if based purely on self-assessment.

In interpreting differences it is important to reflect on the extent of your colleagues' knowledge of you in a work context.

Having looked at the overall picture, it could be helpful to review the individual scales to identify which aspects of your emotional intelligence show the greatest differences in perception. If the differences in ratings are frequently three sten points or more than yours on any scale, this may indicate a need to focus carefully on understanding your level of self-awareness.

Colleagues' Range Profile

The Range Profile Chart below shows the range of views provided by your colleagues. This additional information could help your understanding of the feedback presented so far. If there is a wide range either on the overall EI score or on the elements, then this indicates that your colleagues may be seeing you very differently. It is important to reflect on how well they know you, and for how long they have known you in a work context. If any of the respondents do not know you that well, or have not known you very long, then this may explain some of the differences. Equally, it is important to reflect on the context in which your colleagues know you, and their seniority. For example, if four respondents are your subordinates and one is your boss, this may explain some of the differences.

In reviewing the Range Profile Chart, begin by looking at the overall emotional intelligence result and then the pattern of responses. In general terms a range of two to three stens would indicate some notable differences among respondents, while a range of four or more stens would indicate very significant differences.

Emotional Intelligence Questionnaire: Managerial 360°

Profile Chart Showing the Range of Ratings by Colleagues

Name: Mr Sample

Sten	1	2	3	4	5	6	7	8	9	10	
A	.	.	.	4	5	6	.	.	.	.	Self-awareness
				(1)	(2)	(1)					
B	.	.	.	4	5	6	7	.	.	.	Emotional
				(1)	(1)	(1)	(1)				resilience
C	.	2	.	.	.	.	7	.	9	.	Motivation
		(1)					(2)		(1)		
D	.	2	3	.	.	6	.	8	.	.	Interpersonal
		(1)	(1)			(1)		(1)			sensitivity
E	.	.	.	.	.	6	.	8	9	.	Influence
						(1)		(1)	(2)		
F	.	.	.	.	.	6	7	8	.	10	Intuitiveness
						(1)	(1)	(1)		(1)	
G	.	.	.	.	.	6	7	8	.	.	Conscientiousness
						(1)	(2)	(1)			
EI	.	.	.	.	5	6	7	.	.	.	Overall EI
					(1)	(1)	(2)				

If the range of differences is similar over the majority of the elements, this indicates a relatively consistent pattern of differences in the perception of you by others. However, if range differences arise only on one or two elements, then you might find it helpful to concentrate on understanding why the differences occur on those specific elements.

The profile generated by your colleagues suggests that their perceptions of your emotional intelligence are rather dissimilar. You need to understand why this might be the case before finalising any development actions. If the range of differences is similar over the majority of the elements, this indicates a relatively consistent pattern of differences in the perception of you by others. However, if range differences arise only on one or two elements, then you might find it helpful to concentrate on understanding why the differences occur on those specific elements.

SECTION 3: DEVELOPMENT GUIDELINES

General guidelines

It is possible to develop your overall level of emotional intelligence by planned and sustained development activities. If you wish to develop your capabilities in this area, a useful framework is as follows:

- reflect on, and identify, examples of behaviour which you exhibit in different situations;

- identify those behaviours which are seen as strengths in this report, and develop plans to strengthen and build on these;

- identify those behaviours which are seen as development needs in this report, and identify changes which you could make to address these needs;

- consciously practise reinforcing and changing behaviours, and reflect on your responses to them;

- continuously seek feedback from colleagues on the behaviour you have attempted to change.

Feedback from others

In planning the development of your emotional intelligence, the feedback provided by your colleagues should help you to refine your understanding of your emotional intelligence. However, before responding to the needs identified, if you know who the individuals who responded are, it could be extremely valuable to discuss, in a non-judgemental way, their perceptions with them. This would enable you to focus your development efforts and priorities, and increase your understanding of how others interpret and perceive your behaviours.

The overall development guidelines in your self-report are still important. However, with the benefit of feedback from others you can reflect on how they have perceived your reactions to significant events, challenges or decisions. You could also benefit from discussing your development actions and ideas with colleagues. This will enable you to fine tune your proposed action plans.

Further Reading

Albrow, Martin (1997) *Do Organisations Have Feelings?* London: Routledge.

Bass, Bernard M. (1985) *Leadership and Performance Beyond Expectations.* London: Macmillan.

Belbin, Meredith (1986) *Management Teams.* London: Heinemann.

Collins, James C. and Porras, Jerry I. (1998) *Built to Last.* London: Century Ltd.

Dulewicz, Victor and Higgs, Malcolm (1988) 'Soul Researching', *People Management*, 1 October.

Dulewicz, Victor and Higgs, Malcolm (1999) 'Can Emotional Intelligence Be Developed?', *Leadership and Organisational Development Journal*, Vol 20, Issue 5, August.

Fineman, Stephen (1993) *Emotion in Organisations.* London: Sage Publications.

Goffee, Rob and Jones, Gareth (1998) *The Character of a Corporation.* New York: HarperCollins.

Goleman, Daniel (1996) *Emotional Intelligence.* London: Bloomsbury.

Goleman, Daniel (1998) *Working with Emotional Intelligence.* London: Bloomsbury.

Harris, Thomas A. (1970) *I'm OK – You're OK*. London: Pan Books.

O'Connor, Joseph and Seymour, John (1990) *Introducing Neuro-Linguistic Programming*. London: Aquarian/Thorsons.

Senge, Peter, M. (1990) *The Fifth Discipline*. London: Century Business.